Breaking Away from the Math and Science Book

Physics and Other Projects for Grades 3–12

Patricia Baggett
Andrzej Ehrenfeucht

ScarecrowEducation
Lanham, Maryland • Toronto • Oxford
2004

Published in the United States of America
by ScarecrowEducation
An imprint of The Rowman & Littlefield Publishing Group, Inc.
4501 Forbes Boulevard, Suite 200, Lanham, Maryland 20706
www.scaroweducation.com

PO Box 317
Oxford
OX2 9RU, UK

British Library Cataloguing in Publication Information Available

Library of Congress Cataloging-in-Publication Data

Baggett, Patricia.
  Breaking away from the math and science book : physics and other
projects for grades 3–12 / Patricia Baggett, Andrzej Ehrenfeucht.
     p. cm.
  ISBN 1-57886-085-7 (pbk. : alk. paper)
  1. Physics—Experiments. 2. Physics—Experiments—Methodology. 3.
Physics—Study and teaching (Elementary) 4. Physics—Study and teaching
(Secondary) I. Ehrenfeucht, Andrzej. II. Title.
QC33 .B18 2004
530'.078—dc22

                                                          2003020683

In memory of Richard P. Feynman (1918–1988)

Contents

Preface

An Old School Textbook in Physics

Experimental Science Series

I.

INDUCTIVE

ELEMENTARY PHYSICAL SCIENCE

WITH

INEXPENSIVE APPARATUS, AND WITHOUT
LABORATORY EQUIPMENT

BY

F. H. BAILEY, A.M.

AUTHOR OF "PRIMARY PHENOMENAL ASTRONOMY," INVENTOR OF THE "ASTRAL
LANTERN, OR PANORAMA OF THE HEAVENS," THE "COSMOSPHERE,"
"100 IN 1 PHYSICAL SCIENCE APPARATUS," ETC.

BOSTON, U.S.A.
D. C. HEATH & CO., PUBLISHERS
1897

Here are some quotes from a book, *Inductive Elementary Physical Science, with Inexpensive Apparatus, and without Laboratory Equipment*, by F. H. Bailey, published by D. C. Heath & Co., Publishers, Boston, in 1897. We include them with the realization that over one hundred years ago an author put forth ideas about hands-on experiments with measurements that are very similar to our own.

On the Teaching of Science through Experiments

"No injustice would be done to a teacher if his skill and the educative value of his lessons were measured by his success in making children reason out conclusions from observed facts."

"Teachers who never tried this method (teaching through experiments) will be astonished at the ease with which children adopt it. At first if their previous instruction has been entirely by the memory method (book learning), this one seems to fail completely. The pupils can use neither hands, eyes, nor minds. But I have not yet had a pupil whose habit of learning upon book or teacher was so strong that it did not give way, within a brief space of time, and let some degree of self-activity (and self-reliance) show itself."

"[Y]ou should teach . . . by the most successful method—that of example."

"Children are imitative; and when they see you doing and enjoying interesting experiments, they will wish to do them also."

"This method of studying science furnishes one of the best opportunities for discipline in English composition; for pupils have something to write about . . . and pupils form the invaluable habit of writing upon subjects about which they know something, and expressing their own thoughts and discoveries."

On the Importance of a Special Room (a Laboratory) Where All Equipment Is Kept and Where Most of the Experiments Are Performed

"It is now conceded that the laboratory is one of the first essentials of every well-equipped school, outranking in importance even the library."

A Typical Plan of an Experiment from One School
(Prince School, Boston, principal: Bentley Young)

"The pupils are led, (1) to experiment by themselves, (2) to draw their own conclusions, (3) to write in every case before proceeding farther. (4) They are given an opportunity to interchange opinions (among themselves), (5) arrive at proper conclusions by taking time enough to think over what has been done, and (6) are finally required to write out again their inferences in good English in blank books for inspection and marking."

General Comments for Students (Shortened and Paraphrased)

- Nature is a great teacher but you must ask her questions.
- Experiments are questions you ask Nature.
- Do not skip experiments because they seem too simple. You must see what things are, and not just think what they should be.
- Always experiment carefully and thoughtfully.
- When you see what an experiment teaches, you must tell it in your own language on paper; you must write it.

Acknowledgments

Several years ago we proposed to NASA (National Aeronautics and Space Administration) that we design and implement a university partnership course for prospective and practicing teachers that combined math, science, and technology. We thank NASA and its MASEF (Math and Science Educators for the Future) program for funding the course and the development of materials. This book, our fourth in the Breaking Away series, contains most of the materials used in the course, which has been offered twice in the Department of Mathematical Sciences at New Mexico State University. The course was conceived as an effort to combine experimental aspects of science based on measurement with scientific theory based on mathematics.

Teachers and prospective teachers, enrolled jointly in the same university course, carried out the experiments themselves in the class and then presented them to students in schools. We thank the prospective and practicing teachers, who participated for their enthusiasm in seeing (and feeling) physics in action, and for their willingness to try the units with students. We continue year after year to lend out our tree slices, ostrich eggs, pulleys, magnets, spring scales, and other materials to teachers who took the course and who have made many of the lessons a part of their curricula. Even math graduate students who took the course were excited to make a magnetic vector field, which they had only seen pictures of in a differential equations course. Based on teachers' reports, the curiosity of fourth graders was also piqued by the vector field (as well as other) activities. We are happy that the course, our fifth joint course for pre-service and in-service teachers, will soon be listed in the NMSU catalog.

We are indebted to the administration of the Las Cruces Public Schools for their support, ongoing since 1995, of our partnership courses. In particular, we thank Karin Matray, director of professional development of the Las Cruces Public Schools, and Sandra Nakamura, science and math coordinator, for their unwavering assistance and for helping us to recruit teachers for the courses. We also thank the department of mathematical sciences and its chair, Professor Dave Finston, for encouraging us to develop the courses, and the New Mexico State University College of Education, especially Associate Dean Rick Scott, for making these courses a part of the required curriculum for students planning to be teachers.

Others who provided funding for this project were the New Mexico Collaborative for Excellence in Teacher Preparation (NMCETP) and the NMSU ADVANCE program. We thank them both. We are grateful to Leesa Mandlman and Hiva Javaher for making the illustrations and to Ms. Mandlman for designing the book cover.

Introduction

This book is not meant as a textbook. Rather, it is a collection of science projects that can be carried out in classrooms. The projects are mostly independent of each other, so they do not have to be done in any specific order.

The material is divided into units that are grouped together into chapters. Each unit either describes a problem and an experiment that tries to provide an answer to the question that is posed, or contains some useful background information, mathematical formulas, or general comments.

The experiments can be performed in a classroom or outdoors. They require only resources that are generally available or that can be obtained inexpensively from science catalogs. An experiment forms the core of each lesson. If you cannot have your students actually perform the experiment, we recommend that you skip the topic rather than performing the experiment only as a demonstration or replacing data that students gather by data that are simply given to them. Such data may look the same, but data gathered by students are meaningful to them, and data given by a teacher are not. Each experiment requires careful planning and precise execution. Students always have many questions and need a lot of help, so it is important that teachers do the experiment themselves before trying it in their classrooms.

Numerical calculations should be done with calculators. For some units four-operation calculators are sufficient. Other units require scientific, and occasionally graphing, calculators. We used Excel to graph data from several units, and Internet addresses are provided as sources of additional information for some lessons.

Some units, such as "Tree Rings in Early Grades" and "Magnetic Sand and Patterns with Iron Filings" require only a minimal amount of mathematics or none at all and can be taught to children in the lower elementary grades. Some others, such as "Racing Cars" and "Questions and Answers about Colliding Balls," require higher-level mathematics, namely algebra (including vectors) and sometimes trigonometry (but not calculus). But algebra and trigonometry are not prerequisites for these units. The units have been successfully taught to students for whom the lessons were the first exposure to this level of mathematics. If this is the case, one thing is important: Students need time to absorb new material. If a lesson takes one period in a class of students with strong math backgrounds, then it may take three periods in a class of mathematical novices. But there is a bonus for teaching algebra and trigonometry in the context of experiments. The students never ask, "Why do we need to learn this?"

The easiest lessons have been used as early as in the third grade, and the hardest ones took several periods in high school. In addition, this material has been the basis for a successful one-semester course in mathematics and science for prospective and practicing teachers.

Chapter 1

Lava, Trees, and Ostrich Eggs

Unit 1

Lava

As an introduction, present information to students about volcanic activity and types of lava. Here are some good websites:

> http://www.geology.sdsu.edu/how_volcanoes_work/index.html
> http://www.volcano.si.edu/gvp/
> http://www.nps.gov/havo/visitor/lava.htm

Materials

- Pieces of lava (one per student). (Our lava came from Kilauea on the Big Island of Hawaii. It is lava foam. See pictures.)
- One or two scales per table
- Calibrated beakers with water (for measuring volumes)
- Rulers and wooden blocks for measuring dimensions of the rocks

Task

Each student measures of his/her piece of lava, provides its written description, and draws its sketch (from three points of view).

A good description allows a person to identify this particular piece of rock among all others.

Recommended Procedures

1. Measure and record weight and volume of the rock.
2. Find out how long it is by putting it between two wooden blocks (kept as far apart as possible) and measuring the distance between them.
3. Find out how narrow it is putting it between two blocks (lying as close as possible to each other) and measuring the distance between them.
4. Describe its color, and surface (rough, smooth).
5. Describe its general appearance, and anything that seems unusual.
6. Put it on the table and sketch its outline from the top, front, and side.
7. Try to draw a nice shaded picture.

Measurements and sketches should be made in class. But the final write-up titled "My Rock" can be left as a homework assignment.

Unit 2

Maple Seeds

The seeds of a maple tree are winged. They grow in pairs.

But they usually fall down separately.

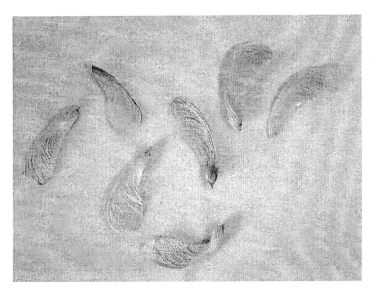

An interesting thing is that when they fall down they turn around like a helicopter blade. They fall slowly, and they can be carried along by the wind for long distances.

Task 1

Give students a collection of winged maple seeds. Let them toss the seeds in the air and observe their flight. Also let them study and draw their shapes and sizes.

Task 2

Make a model of a maple seed using (typewriter) paper for a wing and a small blob of Play-Doh or clay, or a small paper clip, for a seed. The goal is to make it fly just like the real seed does.

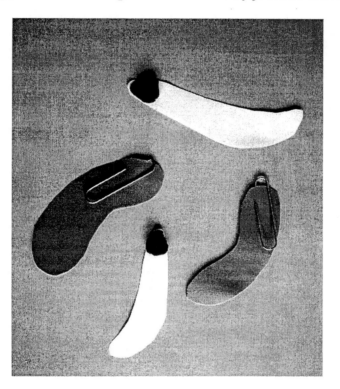

Even the best models will not fly as well as real seeds.

You can measure the quality of your model as follows. Toss it in the air and measure (with a stop watch) the time it takes to float to the ground. The longer the flight, the better the model. This can be made into a class contest.

The task is not easy, but do not give up!

Task 3

Make a maple seed model using Origami.
(See also http://www.grc.nasa.gov/WWW/K-12/TRC/Aeronautics/Maple_Seed.html.)

Andes chocolate wrappers work well to make an Origami maple seed. Instructions for folding are on the next page.

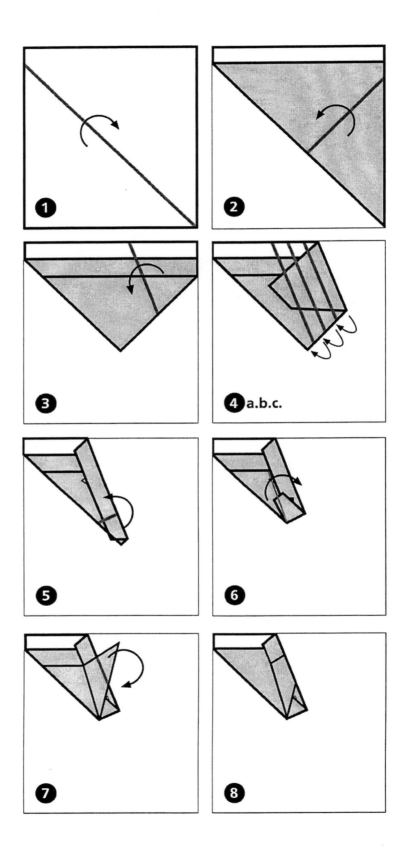

Below we show steps 1 through 8 as they look with an actual candy wrapper.

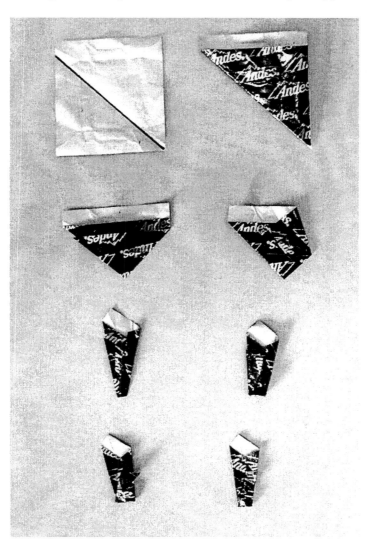

Make your Origami maple seed rotate:

Hold the finished model at the broad end of the wing opposite the weighted seed end, and toss it upward with a flick of the wrist to set it rotating. The model will spin to the ground. Or, to start it rotating on its own, hold it over your head by the broad end, seed end up, and drop it. It should rotate by itself within two feet.

Unit 3

Tree Rings

Students should be provided with background information about the growth of a tree and how tree rings are formed. For some Internet sources, see the following:

http://www-sci.lib.uci.edu/SEP/CTS/TreeRing.html
http://www.valdosta.edu/~grissino/resource.htm
http://www.monroe2boces.org/shared/esp/treering.htm

Tree slices can be bought on the Internet, but the slices we used this unit were donated by a lumber company in Colorado. They are from lodgepole pines and Douglas firs.

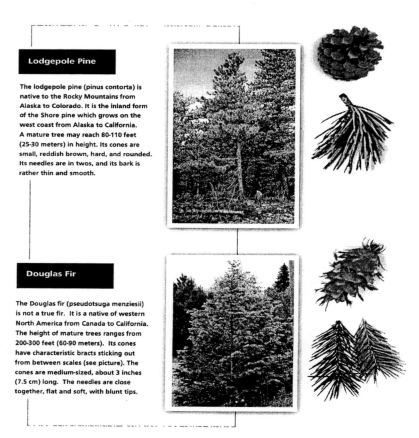

Lodgepole Pine

The lodgepole pine (pinus contorta) is native to the Rocky Mountains from Alaska to Colorado. It is the inland form of the Shore pine which grows on the west coast from Alaska to California. A mature tree may reach 80-110 feet (25-30 meters) in height. Its cones are small, reddish brown, hard, and rounded. Its needles are in twos, and its bark is rather thin and smooth.

Douglas Fir

The Douglas fir (pseudotsuga menziesii) is not a true fir. It is a native of western North America from Canada to California. The height of mature trees ranges from 200-300 feet (60-90 meters). Its cones have characteristic bracts sticking out from between scales (see picture). The cones are medium-sized, about 3 inches (7.5 cm) long. The needles are close together, flat and soft, with blunt tips.

Different Cross Sections of a Tree

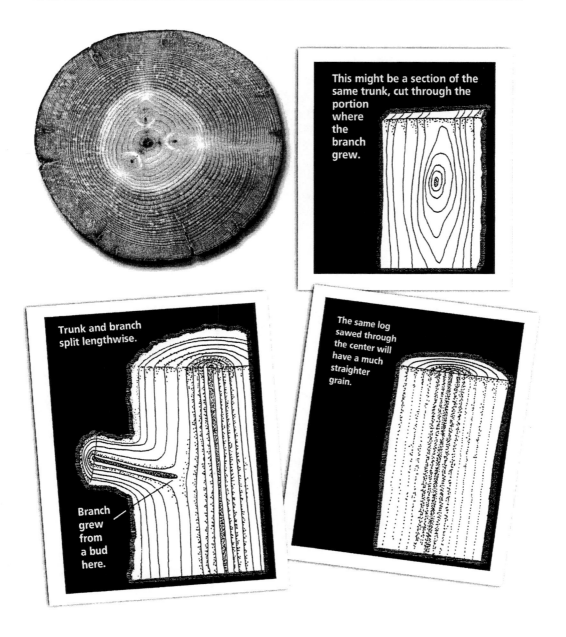

This might be a section of the same trunk, cut through the portion where the branch grew.

Trunk and branch split lengthwise.

Branch grew from a bud here.

The same log sawed through the center will have a much straighter grain.

Not all tree-like plants have rings. For example, bamboo, yucca, saguaro cactus, and palm trees do not have rings. On the other hand, some small bushes, such as rose bushes, have rings.

We will look to see if by studying the tree rings we can tell something about the conditions under which the trees grew.

We are going to measure the rings, analyze the data, and see what conclusions we can draw about the growth conditions of the tree from the data that we analyze.

Question 1

How old was the tree when it was cut? (As far as we know, these trees were cut in 1999.) The main technique to determine the age of a tree is to count the rings. Most trees in tropical, temperate, and northern areas show a yearly growth pattern. The type of the wood, density, and color depend on the growing season. For example, in the far north, trees grow slowly or completely stop growing when the weather is very cold. In the south, trees stop growing when the weather becomes too dry. Each event produces a definite pattern of a tree ring that can be observed, counted, and interpreted. The trees we have are rather young. They were harvested in the Rocky Mountain area.

Method

Individuals may work alone or in groups of two or three. Each person should keep his or her own data sheet.

Materials

- a slice of a trunk of a tree for each group
- needle or pin
- magnifying glass
- ruler
- graph paper
- calculator

Use the pin to keep track of each tree ring as you count it. Count the rings on one side of your slice three times and record the numbers on your data sheet. Now count the rings on the other side of your slice. Are they the same? Why or why not? The slice we used had a maximum of twenty-seven rings on each side. So our tree was planted in about 1972.

Question 2

On average, how much did your tree grow per year? Our slice was 10.1 cm. in diameter, so its radius was about 5 cm. 5 cm. divided by 27 years is about 0.2 cm. (or 2 mm.) per year.

Question 3

We noticed that in our slice, the rings get thinner as the tree gets older. This means that the amount of nutrients becomes more limited. So the rings become larger in circumference but thinner. But suppose that the tree's width increased uniformly each year. Then what would be the area of the new ring each year?

The table below contains such hypothetical data from our tree slice. (We are assuming the radius increases 0.2 cm. per year, namely, that the rings are always the same width.)

	radius in cm.	area of whole cross section = $\pi*r2$ sq cm.	area of new ring = area of whole cross section − area of previous cross section (in sq. cm.)
year 1	0.2 cm.	0.13	0.13
year 2	0.4	0.50	0.37
year 3	0.6	1.13	0.63
year 4	0.8	2.01	0.88
year 5	1.0	3.14	1.13
year 6	1.2	4.52	1.38

Question 4

Look at the growth rate of your tree in different periods of its life. What conclusion can you come to? The graph below shows the rates of growth of our tree in three periods of its life.

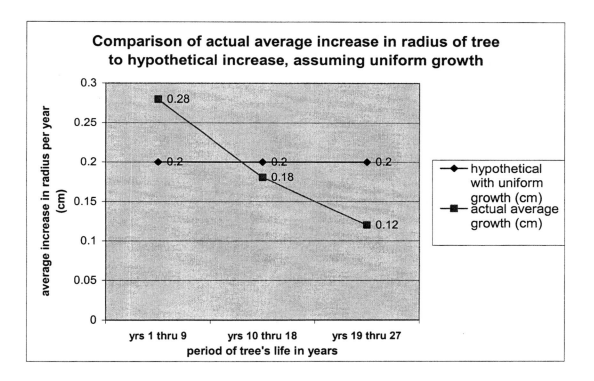

Remarks

1. When we talk about growth, we can measure many different features. In the case of the growth of a tree, we can measure height, radius, diameter, or circumference of the trunk (linear measures in centimeters, meters, inches, or feet). Or we can measure other features such as area of a cross section of the trunk (measured in square units), or volume of a trunk or volume of the whole tree (measured in cubic units). And, of course, this is not all! We choose in this unit as our main feature to look at the areas of one-year growth rings from cross sections of the trunk.

   We observe that the widths of the rings vary from year to year, and we are interested in the pattern of changes. One way of analyzing nonuniform growth is to look at its deviation from uniform growth. This was the reason that we made a table and diagram of the hypothetical uniform growth of a tree with a given number of rings and a given radius of its cross section. That was a preliminary step that created a benchmark to which actual growth can be compared.

2. The math model of a trunk of a tree that is used by lumber companies is a frustum of a very tall and narrow cone (i.e., a cone with its top cut off). This part of a tree provides usable lumber. The volume of wood is calculated from three measurements, the length, the top diameter, and the bottom diameter. What is the formula for computing the volume of a frustum of a cone?

Unit 4

Tree Rings in Early Grades

Most lessons with a substantial hands-on component can be adjusted to different grades. Here is a tree rings activity for early grades.

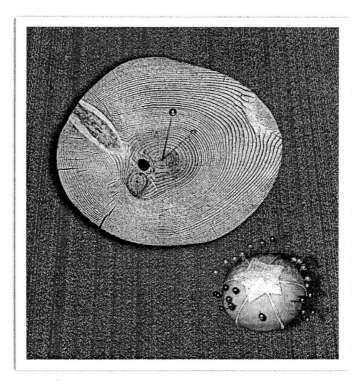

Materials

- Children work in groups of two, three, or four.
- Each group works with one slice of wood with its center marked with a pin. (They may need the teacher's help to find the center and stick in a pin.)
- Each child has one pin to do his or her own counting.

Procedure

1. Children in each group count simultaneously—each child counting in a different direction. After each step they must check that they are on the same tree ring. This will guarantee that the count comes out the same, with the exception of a ring missing at the outer edge because the bark was removed in an uneven way.
2. They can keep track of the count mentally, on a calculator, or in writing.
3. After they finish counting, they measure the radii from the central pin in the direction that they counted, either in centimeters and millimeters, or in inches and sixteenths of an inch.
4. Finally, they prepare a written record in the format shown below. (The record should be handwritten and drawn by the children, and not given as a worksheet.)

Example of a Written Record

Title: Counting rings and measuring radii of a section of a tree.

Measurements:

Name	Count	Radius
Mary	37 rings	8.3 cm.
Juan	37 rings	9.2 cm.
Sue	36 rings	8.1 cm.

Remarks

1. This activity should be accompanied by materials about trees, their growth, and so on.
2. Preparing a report card is an essential part of the activity.
3. All difficult words should be spelled out correctly on the blackboard.
4. The activity described here can easily take more than one class period, but everything should be done the same day.

Unit 5

The Height of a Tree

Introduction

Word problems with scientific content are not science. They are just word problems. Science starts with measurements. In this unit we cover three ways to measure height of a tree. None of the three ways works for tree growing in a forest. The whole tree has to be visible from a distance. The methods also do not work for trees growing on steep slopes or in inaccessible places such as fenced private property. Each method requires that two people collaborate.

First Method

Materials

- long chopstick, skewer, or other straight stick that is long enough
- measuring tape

Task

One person stands at a distance from the tree and aligns his/her stick with the tree, holding the stick at arm's length. The top of the stick must be aligned with the top of the tree, and the thumb of the hand holding the stick must be aligned with the base of the tree. The second person, the helper, waits next to the tree.

Then, without changing position, the person puts the stick horizontally with the thumb still aligned with the base of the tree. The person orders the helper to walk sideways until he/she is aligned with the end of the stick. (It is important for the helper to walk in a direction that is perpendicular to the line from the first person to the tree.) Now the distance from the helper to the tree is equal to the height of the tree and can be measured with the measuring tape.

Second Method

There is a story that the Greek mathematician Thales (640–546 B.C.) astonished the Egyptians by computing the height of the pyramids from their shadows and the shadow of a stick, using similar triangles. The story is probably not true, because the Egyptians knew enough geometry to do more complex tasks. But his method is the most common one used by surveyors. The method requires measuring angles, and surveyors use a piece of equipment called a transit to measure both horizontal and vertical angles. (See the picture of an antique transit on the next page.)

But you need only a measuring tape, a protractor with a hole in its center (most protractors have such a hole), a plumb line made from a heavy nail or small nut hung on a thin string or thread, and a helper.

Tie the plumb line to the center of the protractor. Aim the straight side of the protractor directly toward the top of the tree. Ask you helper to read the angle A between the straight side of the protractor and the vertical plumb line. The helper also should measure the height l of the protractor above the ground while you are still holding it. Finally, both of you should measure the distance d from the place where you are standing to the bottom of the tree.

Schematic Picture

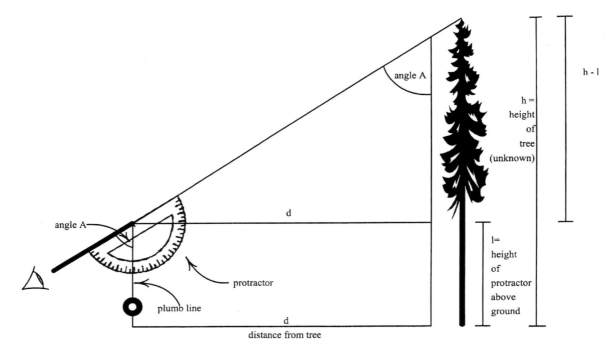

The relationship between the unknown height of the tree h and the measured variables is:

$$\tan A = d/(h - l)$$

So,
$$(h - l)*(\tan A) = d$$

Therefore,
$$h = d/(\tan A) + l$$

Remarks

1. Perform several measurements from a few different positions.
2. Record the data, and do not forget to write down the units.
3. Use a scientific calculator for computations.

Example of one Computation Using the TI-34 II

Data for a Douglas Fir behind My House

angle A	l	d
38°	1.7 m	12.7 m

Enter this expression:
  12.7 / tan(38) + 1.7 ENTER
  17.95525873

Answer: The tree is approximately 18 meters tall.

If you set the calculator to round to 0.1, by [2nd][FIX][1], you would get on the display:
  18.0

Third Method

The height of a tree or building can also be determined using this method:

1. Determine the height of someone in the group.
2. Have the person stand at the base of the tree.
3. Back up far enough to hold a piece of paper at arm's length, and have it be "taller" than the tree, with the base of the tree at the base of the paper.
4. Holding the paper steady (on a clipboard), mark the top of the person's head on the paper and mark the top of the tree on the paper.
5. If the person is six feet tall and you measure his/her height on the paper, you can use it to determine the height of the tree using a proportion.

For example, suppose:

- the person's height on paper is 0.75 inch;
- the tree height on paper is 4.25 inches;
- the person's height is 6 feet;
- and the tree's unknown height is h feet. Then,

$$\frac{.75\text{ in}}{4.25\text{ in}} = \frac{6\text{ feet}}{h\text{ feet}}$$

and

$$0.75 * h = 6 * 4.25$$
$$h = 6 * 4.25 / 0.75$$
$$h = 34 \text{ feet (the height of the tree)}$$

Unit 6

Ostrich Eggs

This unit can be enriched with information about ostriches. Here are some Internet sources:

http://www.ext.nodak.edu/extpubs/alt-ag/ostrich.htm
http://www.nature.ca/notebooks/english/ostrich.htm
http://www.ostrich-birds.com/

The Activity

Finding the volume of an ostrich egg is rather difficult because the egg is large. We will find, as well as we can, the volume of a chicken egg. Then we will find the ratio of the volume of an ostrich egg to the volume of a chicken egg. And these two values will allow us to compute the volume of the ostrich egg. We will also find the weights of an ostrich egg and a chicken egg and their ratios.

Materials

- Students work in groups of four
- Each group needs:
    - an ostrich egg shell (we found inexpensive shells on eBay)
    - several hard-boiled chicken eggs
    - measuring cup or beaker and water
    - ruler
    - two large (5 by 8) index cards
    - paperclips
    - scissors
    - strip of thick paper such as poster board (about 4 inches by 1/4 inch)
    - tape
    - sheet of lined paper
    - pencils
    - scale
    - calculators

Part 1

Find the volume (V) of a chicken egg.

Fill a measuring cup or beaker to some level with water. Record the level. Drop the egg in, and note the new level. Compute the increase in volume. Repeat this several times with different categories of eggs, e.g., small, medium, large, and extra large. Even within the same category, the eggs' volumes can vary. Record your measurements on a data sheet. (Don't forget units!) Find the average volume for extra large, large, and medium eggs (or for the different size categories that you are using).

Part 2

Find the ratio of the volume of an ostrich egg to the volume of a chicken egg of a given size (e.g., small, medium, large, extra large, jumbo).

There are two aspects to this problem. The first one is mathematical—how to express the ratio of two volumes in terms of quantities that we can easily measure, such as the lengths of the eggs and their diameters (or their circumferences). The second aspect is to perform the necessary measurements with adequate precision. We will address both questions below.

Stretching Principle for Areas and Volumes

When a planar figure with area A is stretched, or contracted, in one direction by a factor c, then the new area is c * A. (If $0 < c < 1$, the figure is contracted; if $c > 1$, it is stretched.)

Example

The square abcd below is stretched in direction x by a factor of two. The area of the new figure (the rhombus aecf) is twice the area of the square.

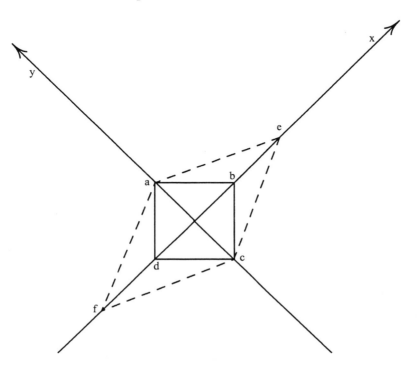

Similarly, when a three-dimensional figure with volume V is stretched in one direction by a factor c, then the new volume is c * V. We can iterate this process. A sequence of stretches (or contractions) by factors c_1, c_2, and c_3 would create a figure with a volume of $V * c_1 * c_2 * c_3$.

We can measure the length and the width of each of the eggs. The width is the same in all directions because the cross section of an egg is a circle.

Let L and W be the length and width of an ostrich egg, and l and w be the length and width of a chicken egg. Let V be the volume of the chicken egg.

Stretching the chicken egg along its length by the factor L/l, and stretching it twice along its cross section with the factor W/w, will lead to a figure matching very closely the ostrich egg, both in size and in shape. Its volume is

> V * (L / l) * (W / w) * (W / w), which we take as an estimate of the volume of the ostrich egg.

Measuring the Length and Width of Eggs (See Pictures)

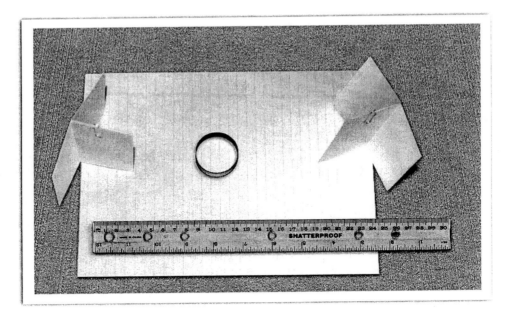

Prepare two index cards to act as delimiters for your eggs. Fold each card into fourths and fasten it with paper clips, as shown in the picture.

Form the strip of thick paper into a circle and fasten it with tape. This circular "stand" will hold your egg while you measure its length and width.

On the lined sheet, draw a straight line down the center, perpendicular to the printed lines.

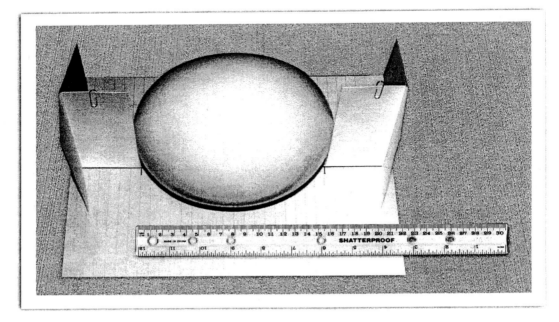

Place the circular holder on the lined sheet, and place one of the eggs (chicken or ostrich) lengthwise on the holder. Line up the two delimiters (index cards) so that they just touch the ends of the egg. With a pencil, mark on the lined paper the positions of the ends of the egg.

Remove the egg, and write ostrich (or chicken) by the marks you made.

Now turn the egg 90 degrees and place it on the holder. Repeat the procedure.

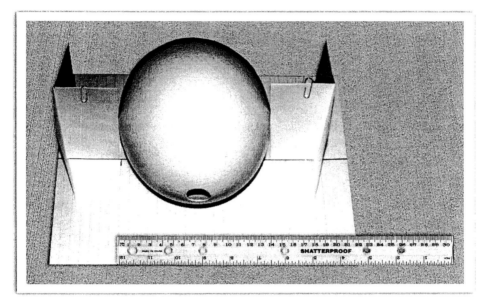

Measure the other egg in the same way. (Don't get your marks mixed up!)

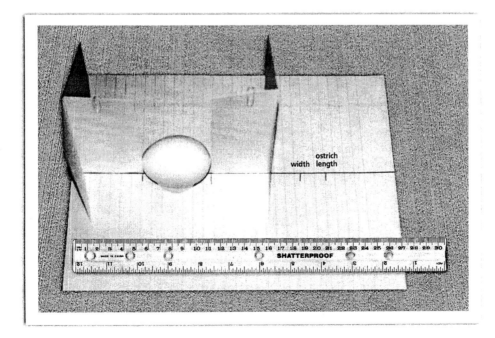

Measure the length between the marks that you made on the lined paper. Here are measurements from our experiment:

	length	width	volume
Chicken egg (extra large)	l = 5.8 cm.	w = 4.5 cm.	V = 60 cu. cm.
Ostrich egg	L = 14 cm.	W = 12 cm.	?

The stretching factors for the three directions are L/l = 14/5.8, and W/w = 12/4.5. So the volume of the ostrich egg is 60 * (14 / 5.8) * (12 / 4.5) * (12 / 4.5) = 1,029.885 cu. cm.

On the TI-108 calculator, the keystrokes are
[60][*][14][/][5.8][*][12][/][4.5][*][12][/][4.5][=].

And the ratio of the volume of the ostrich egg to the volume of the chicken egg is
(14/5.8) * (12/4.5) * (12/4.5) = 17.164751.

Both values should be rounded, so the ostrich egg's volume is 1030 cubic centimeters. And the ostrich egg is about 17 times bigger in volume than the chicken egg.

Part 3

Find the weight of an ostrich egg.

We were only able to obtain empty ostrich eggs, i.e., egg shells. Can we estimate the weight of a full ostrich egg? The density of eggs laid by different birds is approximately the same (slightly more than water), so their weight is approximately proportional to their volume. We can weigh a chicken egg and multiply its weight by 17 to get an approximate weight of an ostrich egg.

Our chicken egg weighed about 2.2 oz. So our ostrich egg weighs about 2.2 * 17.16 = 37.752 oz, or about 2 lb. 6 oz.

Unit 7

Another Way to Find the Volume of an Ostrich Egg
(Using Archimedes' Principle)

Background

Archimedes (287?–212 B.C.) was a mathematician and inventor who lived in Syracuse, Sicily. One thing he discovered has become known as Archimedes' principle, dealing with buoyancy. Buoyancy is the loss in weight an object seems to undergo when it is placed in a liquid. Archimedes' principle states that an object placed in a liquid seems to lose an amount of weight equal to the weight of the fluid it displaces. (In physical terms, a body floating or submerged in a liquid is buoyed up by a force equal to the weight of the liquid displaced.)

The density of an object is its mass divided by its volume, and in the metric system the units for density we often use are grams per cubic centimeter. Water has a density of one gram per cubic centimeter. Objects with densities greater than one sink in water, and objects with densities less than one float in water.

A body denser than water will sink in water because, even when the body is completely submerged, the weight of the water displaced is not as great as the weight of the body itself.

Let's do a hypothetical experiment. Let's suspend a solid gold ball that has a volume of 10 cubic centimeters from a spring scales. Gold has a density of 19.3 grams per cubic centimeter, so the ball should weigh 193 grams. When submerged in water, it is found to weigh only 183 grams. The 10 cubic centimeters of displaced water weighs 10 grams, and this, by Archimedes' principle, is the upward buoyant force exerted by the water.

If the same gold ball were to be made into a hollow sphere with a total volume greater than 193 cubic centimeters, it would float in water.

The Experiment

We noted before that water displacement as a technique to determine the volume of our chicken egg was rather crude. Rather than using water displacement, we will use Archimedes' principle.

Materials

- chicken eggs
- thin string
- spring scale
- beaker with water

Make a "cradle" out of thin string or netting for your chicken egg. Put the egg in the cradle. Set the spring scale to zero. Tie the string from the cradle onto the hook on the spring scale, and weigh the egg in the air. Record the weight; call it weight in air.

Fill a beaker about halfway full with water. With the cradle still attached to the spring scale, lower the egg into the water. Keep the string from the scale to the egg just taut. Do not let the egg touch the sides or the bottom of the beaker. Now record the reading on the scale. Call it weight in water.

Compute the weight in air minus the weight in water. This difference, a loss of apparent weight of the egg, is exactly the weight of the water that the egg has displaced. Therefore, this difference is exactly equal to the volume of the egg measured in cubic centimeters. Since the density of an egg is approximately the density of water, on spring scales that are not very precise this apparent weight (the egg's weight in water) may record as zero. If this is the case, you may take the weight of the egg in grams as the best available estimate of its volume in cubic centimeters.

We can now use this volume, and multiply it by the three stretching factors we found last time, to get a new estimate of the volume of our ostrich egg.

It is best to do this three times, for three different sizes of eggs. Here are our data:

Egg type	length	width	volume V
small chicken	l = 5.8 cm.	w = 4.4 cm.	47 cu. cm.
extra large chicken	l = 5.9 cm.	w = 4.8 cm.	63 cu. cm.
jumbo chicken	l = 7.2 cm.	w = 5.2 cm.	90 cu. cm.
ostrich	L = 15.7 cm.	W = 13.8 cm.	?

New estimate using data from the small egg.
The stretching factors for the three directions are L / l = 15.7/5.8 and W / w = 13.8/4.4. So the volume of the ostrich egg is 47 * (15.7 / 5.8) * (13.8 / 4.4) * (13.8 / 4.4) ≈ 1,251 cu. cm.

New estimate using data from the medium egg.
The stretching factors for the three directions are L / l = 15.7 / 5.9 and W / w = 13.8 / 4.8. So the volume of the ostrich egg is 63 * (15.7 / 5.9) * (13.8 / 4.8) * (13.8 / 4.8) ≈ 1,385 cu. cm.

New estimate using data from the jumbo egg.
The stretching factors for the three directions are L / l = 15.7 / 7.2 and W / w = 13.8 / 5.2. So the volume of the ostrich egg is 90 * (15.7 / 7.2) * (13.8 / 5.2) * (13.8 / 5.2) ≈ 1,382 cu. cm.

How does your new estimate of the volume of the ostrich egg compare with what you got before?

A comment about Archimedes' principle: The loss of weight in grams for a body submerged in water is always equal to its volume in cubic centimeter, independent of its density.

Chapter 2

Some Basic Physics Concepts

Unit 1

Scientific Explanations

Scientific explanations are often very unsatisfactory and disappointing. A beginner in physics often hopes to find the answers to questions such as:

- What is time?
- What is space?
- What are forces?
- What is mass?
- Why do charges that are opposite attract each other, and charges that are the same repel?
- Why does the force of gravity decrease with the square of the distance?
- And many other questions starting with "What is?" and "Why?".

But these questions are not answered. Instead the student is bombarded with equations such as:

- $F = m * a$ (The acceleration of an object caused by a force F is inversely proportional to the mass of the object.)
- $a = dv / dt$ (Acceleration is the derivative of speed over time.)
- $F = g * m1 * m2 /r2$ (The gravitational force between two objects is proportional to the masses of both objects and inversely proportional to the square of their distance apart.)

Such formulas are accompanied by "intuitive" explanations such as:

- When a plane starts, you feel that it is accelerating.
- If you push a heavy object, you feel a force. The object is trying to push you back.

It takes a long time to learn that physics does not try to give answers to questions such as those we asked above, but instead it tries to establish mathematical relationships among measurable quantities. In physics, the explanation of why something happens always has a very narrow meaning, which is simply an explanation of a new phenomenon in terms of formulas that have been derived previously. For example, the kinetic theory of gases explained their physical properties in terms of Newtonian dynamics, which had been developed earlier.

But most students have very little or no experience with scientific measurements, recording data, and comparing results that are predicted by formulas to results that are actually observed. Therefore, relationships among measurable variables are not related to any experience and they remain purely abstract or even empty for a student.

Maybe a proper approach is to concentrate first on measurements and recording data and to bring formulas as a simplification. One formula can briefly summarize patterns of observed values that are otherwise complex and chaotic.

Unit 2

Mass and Weight

Pounds and ounces are units of weight. What kind of units are kilograms and grams? In countries that use the metric system, kilograms and grams also serve as units of weight in everyday situations.

> 1 kg = 2.2 lb, and 1 oz = 28.4 g (approximately)

But in science, kilograms and grams are units of mass, not weight. These two different meanings of 1 kilogram are related in the following way:

> 1 kilogram (in common usage) is the weight of an object that has a mass of 1 kilogram (scientific usage).

Some people try to avoid this confusion by writing 1 Kg and 1 G for weight, and 1 kg and 1 g for mass. But this convention is not widely used.

A scientific unit of weight is 1 newton. An object that has a mass of 1 kg weighs 9.81 newtons. Therefore,

> 1 lb = 4.46 newtons, and 1 oz = 0.28 newton (These conversions are only approximate.) Thus 1 newton ≈3.6 oz.

Newtons are never used in everyday transactions but only in scientific and engineering computations. So you cannot go to a store in Mexico or Canada and ask for 9.81 newtons of sugar. No one would understand what you are talking about.

The system of common measures also has a unit of mass. It is 1 slug, and it is the mass of an object that weighs 1 lb. But no one uses this unit.

In many situations the distinction between mass and weight is not important because these quantities are proportional. An object that weighs twice as much as another object also has a mass that is twice as big, and so on. But mass and weight are two very different attributes of matter.

- Mass is the amount of matter. It remains the same when the object is moved from one location to another one.
- Weight is the result of the gravitational interaction between an object and the rest of the earth.

So if an object is moved from the earth to the moon, its mass remains the same, but its weight decreases because its gravitational interaction with the moon is weaker than it was with the earth.

The other significant difference is that weight is pulling the object down toward the center of the earth. But mass is just some amount of matter, and it doesn't point in any direction.

Gravitational interaction is an example of a force, and all forces are measured in pounds and newtons.

In countries that use the metric system, in practical situations forces are also measured in kilograms (of weight), and this adds to the confusion. For example, pressure is usually expressed in grams per square centimeter, and not in newtons per square centimeter or pounds per square inch.

A confusion between newtons and pounds was the cause of a crash in September 1999 of a probe of the Mars Climate Orbiter, sent to Mars. The landing was controlled by rocket engines. But one team of engineers computed the forces of thrust generated by the engines in newtons, and the other team thought that they were measured in pounds! So the probe crashed. It is hard to believe that no one noticed this discrepancy, which was by a factor of 4.46.

So maybe we need to remind our students more often, "Don't forget to write down the units of measurement!"

Unit 3

Direction of Forces

A force has a magnitude and a direction. When we consider forces that are acting along one straight line, we can represent both the magnitude and the direction of a force by one number. We choose one direction on the line as positive, and represent the forces that are acting in this direction by positive numbers; and we represent the forces that are acting in the opposite direction by negative numbers.

Example

$$\xrightarrow{\hspace{3cm}}$$
1.2

$$\xleftarrow{\hspace{3cm}}$$
-0.7

Forces that act in a plane or in space cannot be described by one number. On the plane we need two numbers to represent one force. Together they describe both the magnitude and the direction.

In space we need three numbers to describe one force. The most common way to describe a force is to choose three mutually perpendicular directions in space (two in the plane) and give the values (which can be negative numbers) of three mutually perpendicular components f_1, f_2, and f_3 of the force f. The list of these components is called a vector and is usually written (f_1, f_2, f_3).

Unit 4

Decomposition of Forces

Very often we need to split a force into two components that are perpendicular to each other. Both of the components, together with the force, are always lying in the same plane. If the angles between the force and its components are A_1 and A_2, and the magnitude of the force is f, then the magnitudes of its components are:

$$f_1 = f * (\cos A_1)$$
and
$$f_2 = f * (\cos A_2)$$

Because $A_1 + A_2 = 90°$, so $\cos A_1 = \sin A_2$, and $\cos A_2 = \sin A_1$.

A geometrical interpretation is shown below.

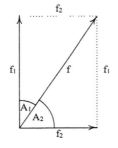

Some basic trigonometry:

$$\sin A_2 = f_1 / f = \cos A_1, \text{ so}$$
$$f_1 = f * \sin A_2$$
$$= f * \cos A_1$$
$$\sin A_1 = f_2/f = \cos A_2, \text{ so}$$
$$f_2 = f * \sin A_1$$
$$= f * \cos A_2$$

Decomposing a force f in space into three perpendicular components can be done as follows: Decompose f into f_1 and f_2, and then decompose f_2 into f_2' and f_2''.

The general case of decomposition into nonperpendicular components is a part of the arithmetic and algebra of vectors. On the TI-83 calculator, vectors are represented by lists. So the arithmetic of lists is really the arithmetic of vectors.

Unit 5

Properties and Interactions

Mass and temperature are properties of matter. But forces are not properties of matter; they occur only as interactions between objects.

If you hang an object on a spring scales, the object pulls the spring down; but also the spring is pulling the object up. An object presses down on a pressure scales, and the scales responds with pushing the object up. These forces can be felt if you use your hand instead of an object to pull or push on the scales. These forces (pulling and pushing) require direct contact between objects, but the force of gravitation acts from a distance. The earth is exerting a force on the moon, and the moon is exerting a force on the earth. It is a mutual attraction. When we observe a force acting on any object, it is always the result of an interaction with another object or the combined effect of interactions with several objects.

Newton formulated this property of forces, saying:

> Whenever one object exerts a force on another, then the second object responds simultaneously by exerting on the first object a force of the same value but in the opposite direction. (This is often called "Newton's law of action and reaction" or "Newton's third law.")

Graphically we can represent forces as arrows whose lengths show the values of the forces (measured in some units such as newtons), and whose directions represent the directions of the forces. Using this method we can illustrate Newton's finding as follows:

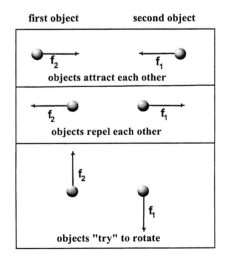

In each case:

- f_1 is the force that the first object exerts on the second object; and
- f_2 is the force that the second object exerts on the first object.

The lengths of both arrows are always the same, but their directions are opposite. Notice that in the last case above the arrows are not lying on the same straight line. This means that we can have many kinds of forces, not just forces that attract and repel.

Remarks

1. The concept of a force changed our thinking about the world around us. We know now that we cannot explain many phenomena in terms of properties of matter because many phenomena depend not on properties of objects, but on interactions among objects.

2. In everyday life people use phrases such as, "This pitcher puts a lot of force on his fast ball," or such as in *Star Wars*, "Let the force be with you." Such expressions indicate that force is considered to be a property that can be possessed and transferred. This use is not in agreement with the concept of force in science.

   The moment that a ball leaves a pitcher's hand, there is no more interaction between the hand and the ball, and therefore no "force" is put on the ball.

   But a fast ball has many properties that are different from a ball that is lying on the ground. For example, a scientist would say that a fast-flying ball has a large kinetic energy, and that the kinetic energy of a ball at rest is zero.

   A scientist would also say that a pitcher gives his fast balls lots of momentum. (Momentum is a different concept than the concept of the moment of forces.)

   This shows that some words used in everyday situations have meanings that are very different from their meaning in science. This confusion of meaning is a very big obstacle to learning science. Even scientifically literate adults often confuse the common meanings of words with their scientific uses.

3. The concepts of kinetic energy and momentum are studied in a domain of physics called dynamics, which deals with the effect of forces on moving objects.

Unit 6

What Is Gravity?

When we weigh an object on a spring scales, we are measuring a force that is called the earth's gravity.

The common view is that the earth's gravity is a force that pulls objects toward the earth's center. Similarly, the moon's gravity pulls objects on the moon's surface toward its center. And in addition, the earth's gravity holds the moon in its orbit around the earth, and the sun's gravity holds the earth and other planets in their orbits.

This view is not wrong; it gives an overall picture of the solar system as a system that is held together by gravity. But in its details it is incorrect, and it often leads to false beliefs such as, "Astronauts get weightless when they stop being influenced by the earth's gravity." (False!)

History

The force of gravity was discovered by Isaac Newton (1642–1727). There is probably no truth to the story that he got the idea while watching an apple fall from a tree. Newton was studying astronomy and looking for explanations for the observed movements of planets and their moons. It happened that his explanation in terms of the force of gravity is very general and explains thousands of other phenomena that happen in the universe, including why it is true that "whatever goes up must come down." His theory was modified by Albert Einstein (1879–1955), but differences in the two theories are at present interesting only for experts in theoretical physics and astronomy, so we will not talk about them.

Let's recall some facts about forces:

- Each force has a magnitude and a direction.
- Forces always come in pairs. If one object pulls another, then it is itself pulled in the opposite direction by another force of the same magnitude.

Gravity is such a pulling force. It operates between *any two objects in the universe that have mass*.

So you may imagine that each atom of your body pulls every other atom in the universe, and therefore it is pulled in the opposite direction. Most of these forces cancel each other or are not observable. But the part we observe and measure by weighing is named the earth's gravitational force. It is really the sum of the forces between the atoms of the weighed object and the other atoms of the earth. The rest either cancel each other or are not observable.

Newton's Formula

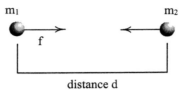

The magnitude f of the gravitational force between two objects is proportional to the product of their masses, m_1 and m_2, and inversely proportional to the square of their distance apart, d:

$$f = c * m_1 * m_2 / d_2$$

The constant c depends on which units are used to measure the forces, distances, and masses. This is a very important formula. It says that the gravitational force does not depend on how objects move or on what is between them. It depends only on their masses and their distance.

Weightlessness

When you dive or are on a roller coaster, you feel (almost) weightless for some brief moments. This feeling is a permanent state for astronauts who are staying in orbit around the earth in a space station or in a space shuttle. Weightlessness is not an illusion. If an astronaut tried to put an object on a spring scale, the scale would show zero weight and the object would probably gently float away.

But the force of gravity is still there, it is just not observable. This is the "free fall" phenomenon.

When a person stands on solid ground, he or she exerts a downward force that is resisted by the ground. This resisting force has a magnitude that is equal to the person's weight, but in the opposite direction (the force of gravity).

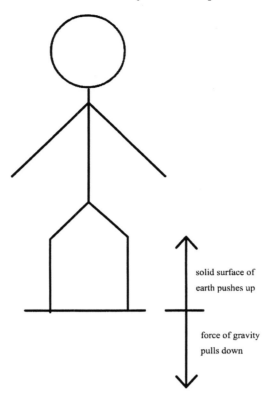

Similarly, the weight of an object on a scale is resisted by a coiled spring.

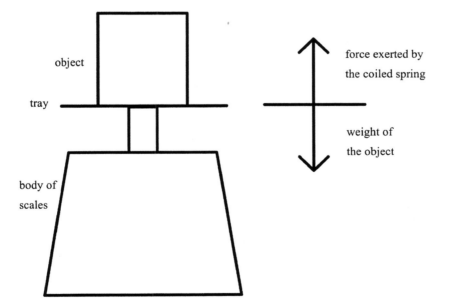

The magnitude of this upward force is displayed by the scale. Thus a scale shows its resistance to a weight (the force of gravity) that has the same magnitude, but opposite direction.

Let's look now at a diver.

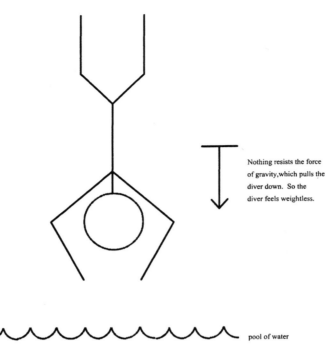

Nothing resists the force of gravity, which pulls the diver down. So the diver feels weightless.

pool of water

This is a general phenomenon. We feel forces when we resist them. Or even more generally, we measure forces by resisting them. Thus there is no measuring equipment which, if placed on a free-falling object, would detect gravity.

Free-Falling, Throwing Stones, and Orbiting the Earth

Remember:

- When all forces that act on an object cancel, then the object either stays motionless or travels along a straight line with constant speed.

What happens when you throw a small heavy object like a rock? What forces act on it when it is in the air? There are only two: gravity and air resistance. But if the object is small and heavy, gravity influences its flight the most, so we will now ignore air resistance.

If there were no gravity, the rock would travel in a straight line in the direction it was thrown. But there is gravity, and no other force opposes it. So the rock is free falling. Its trajectory, shown below, is a smooth combination of two movements. One is a movement in the direction the rock was thrown, and the other is a free fall toward the ground.

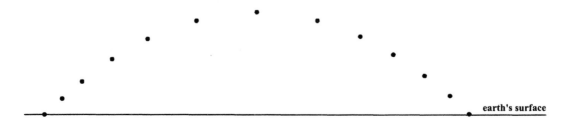

earth's surface

How far the rock will travel depends on its original speed. A rock that is thrown fast will sail farther than a rock that is thrown slowly, if the initial direction is the same.

But the earth is round. So if the rock were thrown fast enough (approximately five miles per second, which is ten times faster than a speeding bullet), then it would not fall at all, but instead it would go into orbit around the earth. And if it was thrown even faster (seven miles per second), it would escape the earth altogether, getting farther and farther away.

Therefore, the movement around an orbit can also be viewed as the combination of two movements—one in the original direction, and the other, which is a free fall toward the earth that is caused by unopposed gravity. Because gravity in a space station is unopposed by any other force, it is not felt and cannot be measured by astronauts.

Remarks about the Space Shuttle

1. Rockets that carry the space shuttle into orbit must take the shuttle above the atmosphere (so there is no air resistance) and reach a speed of five miles per second. Then the rocket may disconnect from the shuttle.
2. The rocket always starts toward the east, in the direction of the earth's rotation. The earth's rotation has a "sling shot" effect on the rocket and makes the task of reaching the required speed easier.
3. When astronauts want to return to earth, they use a small rocket aboard the shuttle to slow it down below five miles per second. This starts their descent. When the shuttle reenters the atmosphere, air drag slows it down to the normal speed of an airplane that is landing.
4. The biggest problem during a shuttle's return is heat. Air drag not only slows down the shuttle, but also heats its surface by friction. So the outer shell of a space shuttle is made from special heat-resistant ceramic plates.

Chapter 3

Stability of a Structure

Unit 1

Designing an Experiment

Steps in Designing an Experiment
1. What is the question we are trying to answer?
2. Design the experiment.
3. Perform the experiment.
4. Study the data gathered from the experiment.
5. Formulate and write down the conclusions.
6. Describe the experimental procedure.

(1) What is the question we are trying to answer? An experiment is an attempt to answer a question.

(2) Designing the experiment. This is the central part of the whole project. The design is dominated by the question of whether the experiment's successful completion could really answer the original question. We have to be realistic. Often, whether we succeed or fail depends on the outcome of the experiment, so we can only say, "We hope to get the answer." Sometimes we can only count on a partial answer or even just some information that will help us to design a new better experiment.

(3) Performing the experiment. Next, the experiment has to be carried out, and all the data have to be carefully recorded and annotated in this step.

(4) Studying the data obtained from the experiment. This is usually the most mathematically intensive part of the whole work. But planning what to do with data should be done during the design part. You should not postpone it until the data are already gathered.

(5) Formulating and writing down the conclusions. This is the part where we go back to the original question and see how successful we were in answering it.

(6) Describing the experimental procedure. In this step we write down a detailed description of the whole procedure and the equipment involved This is often the most lengthy and tedious part. The description should be detailed enough so that others can follow the same procedure and duplicate the results. Usually, in science, we require that an experiment be confirmed by another researcher before its conclusion will be accepted.

Experiments in Classrooms

Teachers must play a very active role in the whole process. Students will need guidance during most steps, so it is essential that teachers perform the experiment themselves before attempting it in class.

Remarks

1. Graduate students who are working toward a degree in science design and perform experiments and analyze data under close supervision of their advisers. They do not have enough knowledge and experience to avoid many pitfalls that can render an experiment useless. It would be naive to assume that elementary, middle, and high school students have enough intellectual maturity to work by themselves on tasks that are so complex and challenging.
2. It is very important that students perform the experiment and record the data themselves. First, watching someone do an experiment and doing it oneself are as different as watching a game or playing a game. Second, it provides equal participation in the project for students of different levels of knowledge and understanding.
3. Students should have ample opportunity to observe each other work and discuss all the issues involved. But the write-up of the conclusions should be done individually.
4. The description of the experimental procedure should be omitted in most cases. It is too tedious, and students rarely are able to do acceptable work.
5. Experiments are time consuming and cannot be rushed. If you can do an experiment in fifteen minutes, give students an hour and don't be surprised if you have to give them still more time.
6. The following is an example of an easy experiment that usually contains some faults.
   - Which paper towel is the best? The towel that absorbs the most water. But it depends on how much of the towel we use. So we can ask about the amount of absorption per roll, per ounce, per sheet, or per square inch. (This ambiguity should be clarified before we start planning the experiment.)
   - The suggested procedure follows. Put some food coloring in water. Use an eyedropper to put some known amount (for example, 6 drops) of colored water on the towel. Measure the size of the stain (either its area, or if the spot is almost circular, its diameter). Evaluate the towels on the basis of the sizes of the stains.
7. What is the problem with this experiment?
8. If we measure a towel's ability to absorb water, we talk about the amount of water that is absorbed by some unit amount of towel, for example, by a square inch or an ounce.
9. We do not have any information about how this ability (to absorb water) is reflected by the size of the stain. It is possible that bigger stains indicate that more water is absorbed by the unit of towel that is used. But it is also possible that the stain is large because the towel's absorption is poor and more area is needed to soak up the water. So without additional information about the relationship between the amount of water that is absorbed and the size of the stain (if such a relationship exists at all), we cannot conclude anything about the original question.

Unit 2

A Conversation about Weight and Mass

What is the difference between weight and mass? Let's listen to a fictitious conversation between a student (S) and a science teacher (T).

S: "Are mass and weight the same?"

T: "No. They are two different concepts."

S: "I weighed this piece of iron. It weighs one pound. What's its mass?"

T: "One pound."

S: "But you told me that mass is different from weight!"

T: "There is no contradiction. Pounds of weight and pounds of mass are different pounds."

S: "I do not understand."

T: "If you went to the moon, your mass would remain the same, but you would weigh less."

S: "I've seen pictures of astronauts on the moon. They didn't lose any weight! They looked exactly like they do on earth."

T: "Yes, because they did not lose any mass. A person gets skinnier by losing mass, not weight."

S: "So what would happen to me if I lost some weight?"

T: "You cannot lose what you don't have."

S: "So, am I weightless?"

T: "No, but your weight is not something you have. Your weight is just a force that pulls you toward the center of the earth. If you were standing on the moon, your weight would be the force that pulls you toward the center of the moon. But the moon has a smaller mass than the earth, so this force is smaller than on earth."

S: "Are you talking about gravity?"

T: "Yes, I'm talking about the force called gravity."

S: "I still do not understand what you are talking about. Maybe because I still do not know what mass is and what forces are. Thinking about it, nobody ever told me what they are. Teachers, such as you, always use these terms as if they were obvious. Can you tell me, in plain English, what mass is, and what forces are?"

T: "No, because basic concepts that are used in physics such as mass or force are never defined. They are introduced in one of two ways, either by telling how to measure them, or by telling how to compute them from some other measurements."

S: "Okay, so tell me how to measure mass and forces."

T: "Mass is always computed from other measurements. And the simplest tool for measuring forces is a spring scale, on which you can hang something you want to weigh.

Spring scales are good because they can also be used for pulling objects in different directions. And we will need at least two of them, together with some string that is light and strong, and some objects that are rather heavy but still easy to handle, like steel nuts." (See the picture showing one type of spring scale.)

S: "So the forces will be just the numbers I read from these scales?"

T: "Yes. Would you like to start now?"

Unit 3

Feeling Forces

Materials

- spring scale (one for every two students)
- a large selection of objects to weigh

Task

Hang the scale from your finger. Then hang an object on the scale and guess its weight in ounces (or grams of weight). Let your partner read the real weight. Record the results. Repeat this many times. Change roles with your partner. Are you getting better at guessing?

Discussion

Topic: Forces Are Interactions between Objects

(1) What forces act on the object that is weighed?
- Its weight, which is a gravitational interaction between the object and the rest of the earth. The weight pulls the object down.

- The pull of the hook of the scales upward. This pull is a force of the same strength as the weight of the object, but directed in the opposite direction.

(2) What forces act on the spring scales?
- Its own weight.
- The weight of the object, which pulls the hook down.
- The pull of your finger upward, which balances the sum of the weight of the scale and the object.

(3) What force do you feel?
- The downward force, which is the sum of the weights of the scales and the object being weighed.

Unit 4

Weight Is a Force

Students work in groups. They need two small kitchen spring scales per table.

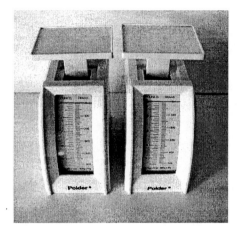

Preparation

Take off the movable trays and adjust the scales so that they show "0" without the trays. (You will not use the trays in this unit.) Check the scales for uniformity and accuracy.

Task 1

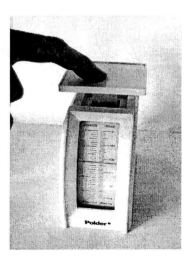

Press one scale with one finger until it registers 8 ounces and hold it at this point. Do the same thing several times but now hold the scales horizontally and in other positions.

Repeat this a few times, trying to get different target values: 3 ounces, 12 ounces, and so on, just by feel.

So we are learning two things:
1. Forces are measured in the same units as weights.
2. Forces have directions (you were pressing your finger down, sideways, and maybe even straight up).

Task 2

How much does your scale weigh?

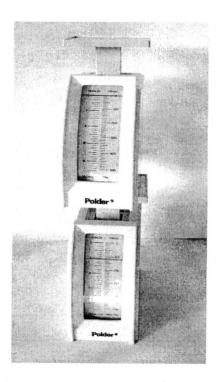

You have two scales on your table, so just put one on top of the other. (My scale weighs 4 ounces.)

Set a scale upside down, and read the value. This makes the scale weigh itself! (On my scale I read 2¼ ounces.) What does it mean?

The scale contains a body (which weighs b ounces), and a movable top (which weighs t ounces). In the upright position the top presses down on the spring and the scale records 0 ounces for the weight of t from the top.

In the upside down position the body presses on the spring and the scale shows 2¼ ounces for the weight of b from the body.

Thus, b − t = 2¼ ounces. But the total weight is b + t = 4 ounces. So b = $3\frac{1}{8}$ ounces and t = $\frac{7}{8}$ ounces.

Task 3

Here is a question: Who was pushing whom? Did your finger push the scale, or was the scale pushing your finger?

Put the two scales on their sides with their stationary trays touching. Push one of the scales with the other scales. What are the readings? Both scales show the same reading!

So when your finger was pushing the scale, the scale was pushing your finger with a force of the same magnitude but in the opposite direction.

Remark

1. This fact, that all forces always come in pairs of the same magnitude but opposite direction, was discovered by Isaac Newton, and it is the most important fact about forces. Forces are usually drawn as arrows whose length represents their magnitude.

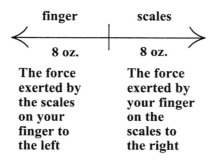

finger   scales

8 oz.   8 oz.

**The force
exerted by
the scales
on your
finger to
the left**

**The force
exerted by
your finger
on the
scales to
the right**

The point where your finger and the scale touch each other is in the middle.

Task 4

Take a rubber band, cut it to make one strand, and stretch it using both hands. Draw a picture (such as the one above) showing what is happening. Don't forget that you are pulling the rubber band and not pushing it!

Solution

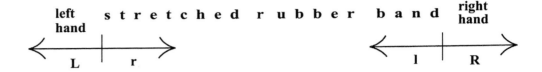

All four forces have the same magnitude.
- "L" is the force exerted by your left hand on the rubber band.
- "R" is the force exerted by your right hand on the rubber band.
- "r" the rubber band pulls your left hand to the right.
- "l" the rubber band pulls your right hand to the left.

Unit 5

Distribution of Weights

Materials

Students work in small groups. Each group needs:
- two pressure scales
- a set of blocks made from one cubic inch cubes with lengths from one to ten inches
- several single cubes
- and graph paper with a one square centimeter grid

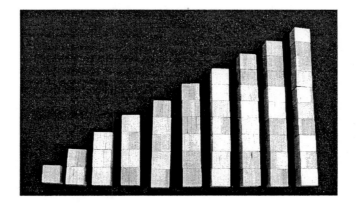

Preliminary Activities

Students learn to use scales, weigh the blocks in both ounces and grams, and record the weights.

Example of a Record

Number of cubic inches in a block:	the block's weight	
	grams	ounces
1	10	0.35
2	19	0.65
3	30	1.05

Task 1

Put two scales side by side and place a single block on each scale. Build one structure supported by both blocks, adding one block at a time. Record the weight on each of the scales after each block is added. Draw a side view of the structure on the graph paper with a square grid, showing the order in which it was built. Check that the sum of the weights that is shown on the two scales always equals the total weight of the blocks you are using. Here is an example:

Scale has	Readings on	
	scale 1	scale 2
No blocks	0	0
Block 1 is added (2 cubes)	19	0
Block 2 is added (4 cubes)	19	41
Block 3 is added (10 cubes)	60	105
Block 4 is added . . .		

Task 2

Make a structure such that adding the next block decreases the weight shown on one of the scales.

Example

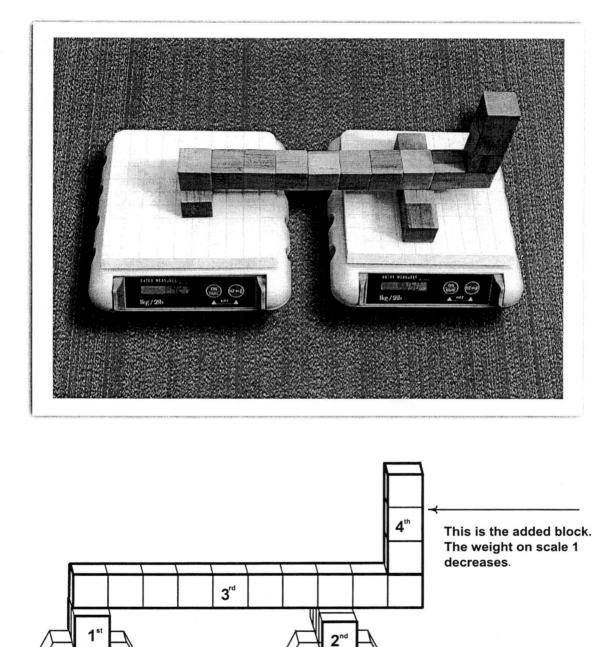

This is the added block. The weight on scale 1 decreases.

(Do not show this example until the students find their own solutions.)

Unit 6

Examples of Computations of the Stability of a Structure

Introduction

There are many methods to predict the stability of a structure. Analyzing complex structures such as bridges, tall buildings, and so on can be very difficult. We will show only two simple examples.

Example 1

You will need your cubic-inch columns of blocks for this task. Build the construction shown below, adding one block at a time, beginning with the three-cube block. Be precise; align the blocks as shown. After how many blocks will the structure topple over? Predict first, and build later!

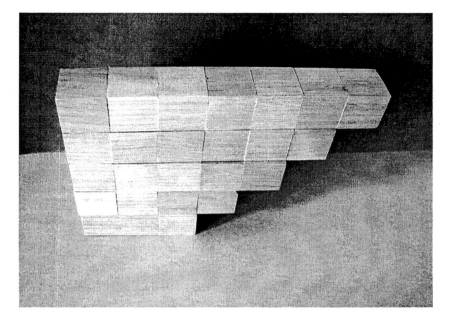

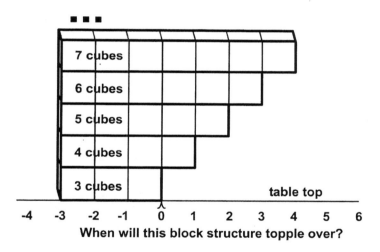

When will this block structure topple over?

The prediction is based on the assumption that all the cubes that were used in making the three-cube block, the four-cube block, and so on are of the same size and weight. (The unit used in measuring weight is the weight of one cube.) This prediction is only approximately true, so the experimental results may be different from the computed result.

The construction topples when the center of gravity of the structure standing on the top of the three-cube block (the three-cube block is the support of the whole structure) falls to the right of its end marked by the caret (^) shown in the picture above.

Put a scale on the horizontal line using the caret as the 0 point and the unit as the length of a cube. (See the picture above.)

The center of gravity of each block is in its middle, so:

Block	Its center x_i is above	Its weight w_i
4-cube	−1.0	4
5-cube	−0.5	5
6-cube	0	6
7-cube	0.5	7
8-cube	1.0	8

The center of gravity of a structure built from k blocks whose centers of gravity are above $x_1, x_2, \ldots x_k$, and whose weights are $w_1, w_2, \ldots w_k$, is above:

$(x_1 * w_1 + x_2 * w_2 + \ldots + x_k * w_k) / (w_1 + w_2 + \ldots + w_k)$. (This is simply a weighted average.)

Therefore,

Structure with blocks	Position of its center of gravity
4-cube	(−1 * 4) /4 = −1
4- , 5-cube	(−1 * 4 + −0.5 * 5) / (4 + 5) = −0.72
4- , 5- ,6-cube	(−4 + −2.5 + 0) / 15 = −0.43
4- , 5- , 6- , 7-cube	(−4 + −2.5 + 0 + 3.5) / 22 = −0.14
4- , 5- , 6- , 7- , 8-cube	(−4 + −2.5 + 0 + 3.5 + 8) / 30 = 0.17

Thus, adding the eight-cube block will topple the structure. (See picture below.)

But don't be surprised if your structure topples after the seven-cube block is added!

Example 2

Build the structure shown below. It is supported by a one-cube block and a two-cube block. (The two-cube block is placed vertically.) On these two blocks you have a six-cube and a nine-cube block. And at the top you have two blocks put crosswise, one X-cube block and one Y-cube block (if you prefer, you may omit one or both of these, by making X or Y = 0). For what X and Y is the structure stable? (If you prefer, you may add an extra block on the top of the Y-cube block.)

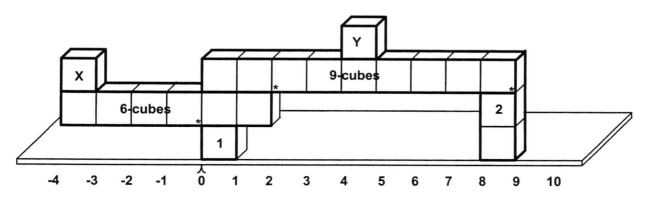

The only way the structure can topple is when the left end of the six-cube block starts falling down. If this happens, the contact among the one- , six- , nine- , and two-cube blocks is limited to the points marked by asterisks. The critical factor that decides the stability is the moment of forces acting on the six-cube block relative to the asterisk marked by the caret below. The weights of the nine- and Y-cube blocks are distributed between the two points marked by the two other asterisks; the left one is contributing to the moment acting on the six-cube block. As in the example above, we choose as the 0 point the point marked by the caret; and as the unit of length, we choose the length of one cube. As before, the weight of one cube is computationally irrelevant (because it cancels out), providing that all cubes weigh the same.

(1)   Distribution of weight of the nine- and Y-cube blocks between the two points marked by an asterisk. Their center of gravity is 2.5 units to the right of the left asterisk and 4.5 units to the left of the right one; their weight is 9 + Y. Thus, the force pressing on the left point marked by an asterisk is

(9 + Y) * 4.5 / (2.5 + 4.5) = (9 + Y) * 4.5 / 7 = 81 / 14 + 9/14 * Y
(This is worked out in the footnote on page 70.)

(2)   Computation of the moment of forces acting on the six-cube block.

Three elements contribute to the moment relative to the support point marked by the asterisk. (The unit for a moment is measured by the weight of one cube times the length of the edge of one cube.)

Block	Weight	Position on horizontal line	Moment M = weight * distance
X-cube	X	–3.5	–3.5 * X
6-cube	6	–1	–6
other force (from 9- and Y-cube blocks)	81/14 + 9/14*Y	2	81 / 7 + 9 / 7 * Y

Total moment M = 39 / 7 – 3.5 * X + 9 / 7 * Y

The construction is stable if M > 0 (the bigger the better). When M = 0, there is a "precarious" balance (which is not acceptable from an engineering point of view). The construction topples if M < 0. Therefore, for the construction to be stable:

39 / 7 – 3.5 * X + 9 / 7 * Y > 0

Solving for Y:

9 / 7 * Y > 3.5 * X – 39 / 7
Y > 7 / 9(7 / 2 * X – 39 / 7)
Y > 49 / 18 * X – 39 / 9

Substituting in some values for X gives the following table of minimal values for Y that will make the structure stable:

X	Minimal value of Y	Rounding Y up to a whole number
0	–4.3	0
1	–1.6	0
2	1.1	2
3	3.8	4
4	6.6	7
5	9.3	10

So when X = 4, Y needs to be greater than or equal to 7 in order for the structure not to topple. See the picture below, showing X = 4 and Y = 7.

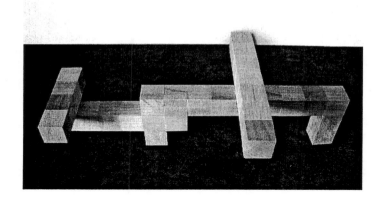

When X = 4 and Y is only 3, the structure topples! See below.

When X = 5, Y needs to be 10 or larger in order for the structure to balance. Below, Y = 7, so the structure topples.

Try some of these values for X and Y with your structure to see how close they are!

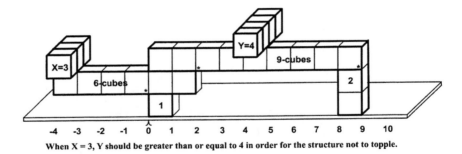

When X = 3, Y should be greater than or equal to 4 in order for the structure not to topple.

Footnote

Here we show how to compute the force pressing on the left point marked by an asterisk, namely, w1 in the figure below.

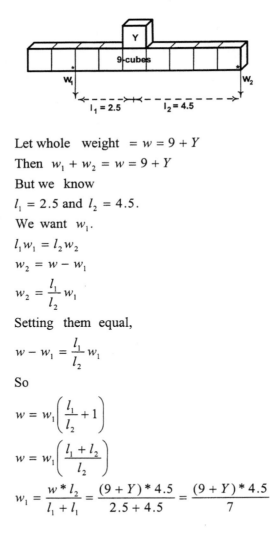

Let whole   weight $= w = 9 + Y$

Then $w_1 + w_2 = w = 9 + Y$

But we   know

$l_1 = 2.5$ and $l_2 = 4.5$.

We want w_1.

$l_1 w_1 = l_2 w_2$

$w_2 = w - w_1$

$w_2 = \dfrac{l_1}{l_2} w_1$

Setting them equal,

$w - w_1 = \dfrac{l_1}{l_2} w_1$

So

$w = w_1 \left(\dfrac{l_1}{l_2} + 1 \right)$

$w = w_1 \left(\dfrac{l_1 + l_2}{l_2} \right)$

$w_1 = \dfrac{w * l_2}{l_1 + l_1} = \dfrac{(9 + Y) * 4.5}{2.5 + 4.5} = \dfrac{(9 + Y) * 4.5}{7}$

Unit 7

More on the Distribution of Weights

Materials

Students work in small groups. Each group needs:
- two pressure scales
- a ruler
- two chopsticks or pencils
- calculators
- and two heavy metal nuts of different weights

They set up an experiment as follows:

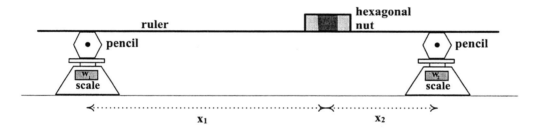

Experiment 1

1. Prepare a data sheet. (See sample data sheet on the next page.)
2. Use the tare button to subtract off the weight of the ruler and pencils.
3. Put a nut on the ruler.
4. Measure and record the distances x_1 and x_2 on the ruler from the middle of the nut to the left and right pencils.
5. Record the weights w_1 and w_2 on the left and right scales.
6. Repeat this at least ten times with the nut placed in different positions.
7. Measure the distance in centimeters and the weight in grams (of weight); convert the weights to newtons. One gram (of weight) = 0.00981 newtons. You may round it to 0.01 newtons.
8. For each measurement, compute $w_1 + w_2$, $x_1 * w_1$, and $x_2 * w_2$.
9. Write the units correctly. The products are called moments of forces and are measured in newtons times centimeters (newton * cm.).
10. Observe that $w_1 + w_2$ remains constant, and that $x_1 * w_1 = x_2 * w_2$. (If it doesn't, check your experimental setting.)

Experiment 2

Repeat experiment one with the second nut (which has a different weight).

Experiment 3

Now put both nuts on the ruler at the same time and record their positions and the readings on the scales. How do they relate to the readings for a single nut? Try to formulate some conclusions. Be precise!

Sample data sheet using one nut (these are actual data).

| measure-ment number | distance of nut from pencils | | weight in grams | | weight in newtons (1 g ≈ .01 newton) | | Total weight w_1+w_2 in newtons (N) | moments of forces | |
	$x_1 =$ distance from left pencil	$x_2 =$ distance from right pencil	$w_1 =$ wt on left scale (g)	$w_2 =$ wt on right scale (g)	$w_1 =$ wt on left scale (N)	$w_2 =$ wt on right scale (N)		$x_1 * w_1$ in newton * cm.	$x_2 * w_2$ in newton * cm.
1	6 cm.	14 cm.	22 g	9 g	0.22 N	0.09 N	0.31 N	1.32 N * cm.	1.26 N * cm.
2	10 cm.	10 cm.	15 g	16 g	0.15 N	0.16 N	0.31 N	1.5 N * cm.	1.6 N * cm.
3	0 cm.	20 cm.	30 g	0 g	0.30 N	0 N	0.30 N	0	0
4	2 cm.	18 cm.	27 g	3 g	0.27 N	0.03 N	0.30 N	0.54 N * cm.	0.54 N * cm.

Unit 8

Predicting the Location of the Center of Gravity

(An example is worked out at the end of this unit.)

Materials

Students work in pairs. Each pair needs:
- one pressure scale
- a wooden ruler or a ruler made of stiff plastic
- several wooden blocks that can be used to construct a "pillar" of the height of the top of the scales
- two short pencils
- a selection of rocks, iron nuts, and other objects that can be used as weights

Task

Each student weighs and records the weights of the ruler and the other objects.

Then one student sets up the basic design, which consists of the scale, a pillar made from wooden blocks, and a ruler supported at both ends by the scale and the pillar. Putting pencils between the ruler and its support pinpoints the exact points of the support.

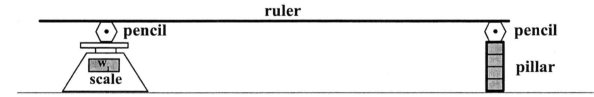

Now the second student arranges some of the objects on the ruler. The first student, after reading the scale, has to find a position under the ruler such that the whole construction can be supported by just one block one inch wide; put it there under the ruler.

Students change roles and repeat this process a couple of times. Calculations should be done with calculators.

Solution

Add the (already recorded) weights of the ruler and the objects on the top of the ruler, and call this total weight W. (You can use the tare button on the scale to subtract off the weights of the pencil and/or the ruler if you wish, but be careful in your computations to take into account what is and isn't included in the weights.)

If the weight showing on the scales is W_1, then the weight pressing on the pillar is:

$$W_2 = W - W_1$$

So if the horizontal distance from the scales to the center of gravity is L_1, and the horizontal distance from the center of gravity to the pillar is L_2, then

$$W_1 * L_1 = W_2 * L_2 \text{ (the moments of forces are in equilibrium)}$$

And of course $L_1 + L_2$ is the known distance between the two pencils supporting the ends of the ruler. These two equations allow you to find L_1 and L_2 with sufficient precision to support the whole arrangement on a block one inch wide and to remove both the scales and the pillar without disturbing the arrangement.

Example

Before starting, I weighed a piece of quartz: 103 grams; and two hexagonal nuts: 31 grams each. I set up the equipment with pencils, ruler, and scale. For convenience, I made the distance between the pencils 24 cm. (My ruler touched the pencils at 3 cm. and 27 cm.) I used the tare button on the scale to take off the weight of the pencils and ruler, so my scale read zero. I put the quartz and two nuts on my apparatus. I want to find the center of gravity of my ruler. (See diagram below.)

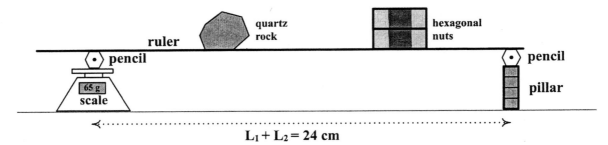

$$L_1 + L_2 = 24 \text{ cm}$$

L_1 = horizontal distance from left scale to center of gravity
L_2 = horizontal distance from center of gravity to blocks.
I don't know L_1 or L_2 yet, but $L_1 + L_2 = 24$ cm.

Item	Weight
Quartz rock	103 grams
Nut	31 grams
Nut	31 grams
Total weight W	165 grams

The reading on the scale is 65 grams = W_1.
The weight pressing on the pillar of blocks = $W_2 = W - W_1 = 165 - 65 = 100$ grams.
We now have two equations in two unknowns, L_1 and L_2:

     (1) $W_1 * L_1 = W_2 * L_2$
     (2) $L_1 + L_2 = 24$

From (1), since $W_1 = 65$ and $W_2 = 100$,
$65 * L_1 = 100 * L_2$
$L_1 = 100 / 65 * L_2$
From (2), substituting $100 / 65 * L_2$ for L_1,
$100 / 65 * L_2 + L_2 = 24$ cm.
$165 / 65 * L_2 = 24$, so
$L_2 = (65 / 165) * 24 = 9.45$ cm.

So the center of gravity is approximately at $27 - 9.45 \approx 17.5$ cm. on the ruler. (This is $14.55 / 24 * 100 = 60.625\%$ of the length between 3 and 27 cm., beginning from the 3 cm. mark on the ruler.)

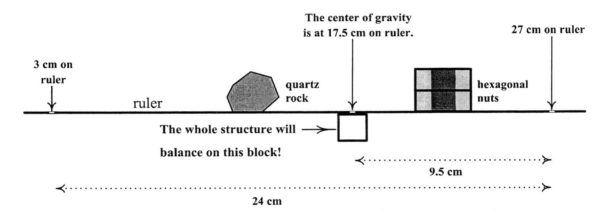

I take a cubic inch block a slide it under this point on the ruler, and voilà, I can pick it up! It balances! When we did this in class, one student took just a pencil (not a cubic inch block) and slid it under the 17.5 cm. point on the ruler. It balanced with only the pencil as support!

Chapter 4

Friction

Unit 1

What Is Friction?

Friction is a force opposing the motion of an object that may slide over the flat surface of another object. The magnitude of the force you need to exert on the object to start its motion is called static friction.

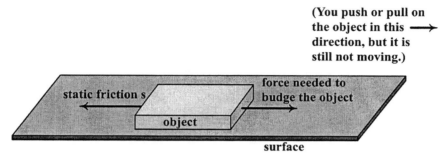

When the object is already moving, the force that pulls in the direction opposite to the direction of the movement is called kinetic friction. If kinetic friction is not neutralized by an opposite force, the object slows down and eventually stops.

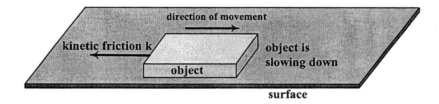

For small speeds, the magnitude of the kinetic friction between a moving object and the surface is always smaller than or equal to the static friction, although usually the difference between static and kinetic friction is small. But kinetic friction may depend on the speed in an irregular way, so the picture becomes very complex.

Here we are not talking about objects that are rolling or tumbling. When this happens, the resistance to movement can become very small.

Here are some basic facts about kinetic friction at small speeds.

- Friction is proportional to the force that a moving object exerts on the surface. If the surface is horizontal, the frictional force, which is always perpendicular to the surface, is simply the weight of the object.

Example

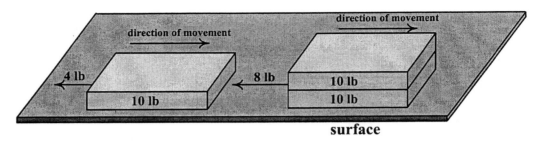

- Friction is (almost) independent of the surface area of contact of the object with a (hard) surface.

Example

If we have a brick with dimensions 5 cm by 10 cm by 20 cm, the friction between it and the surface on which it is moving is (almost) the same in all three positions.

The friction is almost the same in all three positions.

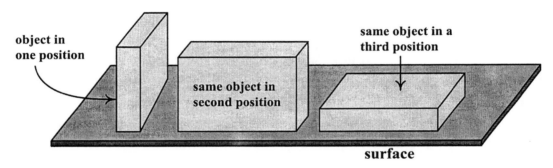

- The magnitude of friction depends on the chemical composition of both the object and the surface, and on some properties of the contact area, such as roughness.

Example

The friction between a 1 lb *wooden* brick sliding on a glass surface is different from the friction between a 1 lb *glass* brick sliding on the same surface.

Coefficients of Friction F_s and F_k

The ratios of the magnitudes of static and kinetic friction, s and k, to the magnitude of the force f exerted by the object on the surface it is standing on or moving on, are called coefficients of static and dynamic (kinetic) friction, F_s and F_k:

$$F_s = s / f, \text{ so } s = F_s * f \qquad\qquad F_k = k / f, \text{ so } k = F_k * f$$

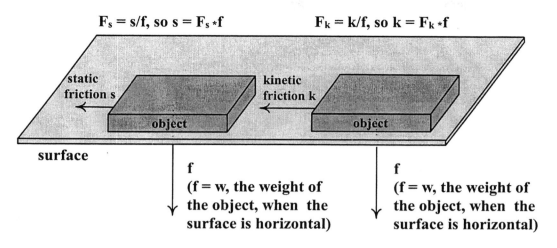

$F_s = s/f$, so $s = F_s * f$ $F_k = k/f$, so $k = F_k * f$

static
friction s

kinetic
friction k

object   object

surface

f
(f = w, the weight of
the object, when the
surface is horizontal)

f
(f = w, the weight of
the object, when the
surface is horizontal)

Example

If $s = 8$ lb, $k = 6$ lb, and $f = 12$ lb, then $8 = F_s * 12$ and $6 = F_k * 12$. So, the coefficient of static friction, $F_s = 0.67$, and the coefficient of kinetic friction, $F_k = 0.5$.

Notice that these coefficients are abstract numbers (they do not have "physical dimensions" measured in some physical units).

Coefficients of friction are important. Let's assume that I want to know the force of static friction of a block of concrete weighing 20 tons, standing on a horizontal concrete base. In the lab I measure that the static friction between a 1 lb block of concrete standing on a concrete base is 9.5 oz. Thus, $F_s = 9.5/16 = 0.59$. Therefore, the friction between a 20 ton block and its base will be $0.59 * 20 = 11.8$ tons.

Coefficients of friction that are typically encountered are between 0.2 and 1. Values that are even lower can be obtained by lubricating a surface with grease, oil, or even mud made out of clay. Higher values are obtained by choosing the proper chemical composition of the object (an example is car tires).

Remarks about Friction

Whenever we see an object already moving, even very little, we know that we have already overcome static friction. Therefore, the coefficient of kinetic friction F_k cannot be greater than the coefficient of static friction F_s. Thus:

$$F_k \leq F_s$$

We observe this in many situations. On slippery ground, it is better not to start sliding; it is hard to stop sliding. When you are already moving, the friction is smaller. The same is true with a skidding car. It is easier to prevent skidding than to recover from it. There is a big difference in the static and dynamic coefficients of friction in the wax that is used on cross-country skis. The wax can hold you when you climb, but it slides well when you ski down.

But the difference between F_k and F_s is usually very small and cannot be detected in simple experiments with equipment that is not very precise. So in many situations we just talk about the coefficient of friction, without differentiating between F_s and F_k.

Each coefficient of friction is the ratio of two forces, but notice that they are perpendicular to each other. Friction is parallel to the surface, and the force pressing the object to it (usually a component of gravity) is perpendicular to the surface on which the object is sliding.

The force that must be overcome to *start* an object's motion is static friction. The force that must be overcome to *keep* the motion is dynamic friction.

Measuring F_s and F_k (a Hands-On Activity)

Coefficients of friction are very easy to measure. The only equipment you need is a protractor!

Theory

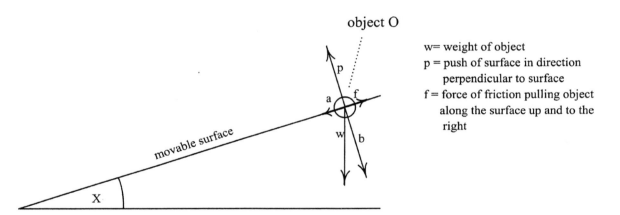

object O

w = weight of object
p = push of surface in direction perpendicular to surface
f = force of friction pulling object along the surface up and to the right

If an object O stays without moving on a surface inclined to the horizon by angle X, there are three forces acting on it that add up to zero (see diagram).

The three forces are its weight w, pulling it straight down; the pushing upward of the surface, p, in the direction perpendicular to the surface; and the force of friction f pulling it along the surface up and to the right.

We can see this better if we look at w as the sum of two forces, a and b. Force a pulls the object downward to the left along the surface, and force b, perpendicular to a, presses the object down and to the right, toward the surface.

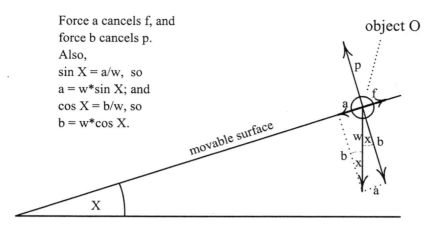

Force a cancels f, and force b cancels p. In addition, a = w * sin X, and b = w * cos X.

Thus, if we find the biggest angle X such that object O still stays in place (which means that any increase of X would make it slide down), then for this angle, the force f (f has the same magnitude as a), is the static friction (and b is the force that presses on the inclined surface).

So F_s = f / b = a / b = (sin X) / (cos X) = tan X

Similarly, if we find the smallest angle X such that the object stays in place, but whenever we give it a small push to start moving, it will slide down to the bottom, then F_k = tan X. Note that when tan X ≥ 1, this means X $\geq 45°$, so the object should slide.

Example

The biggest angle for which the object stays in place on its own is 35°; tan (35°) = F_s = 0.70. The smallest angle for which a small push sends the object all the way down is 32°; tan (32°) = F_k = 0.64.

Task

Measure the coefficients of friction for several objects on one surface.

Students work in teams. Each team needs one movable surface on a table, a protractor, a scientific calculator to compute the tangent of X, and a large collection of objects that are not round.

There are many movable surfaces that are easily available. Some of the best are made of corrugated cardboard in the form of display boards; but surfaces made from cardboard boxes will do. You may increase the thickness and strength of your surface by fastening together two layers of cardboard with packaging tape. Wooden boards with different finishes are also nice. We also used glass, sand paper on cardboard, and linoleum. Boards as small as 7 by 14 inches can be used, but boards measuring 1 by 2 feet are better.

Use packaging tape to attach one end of the board to the table, and put a stack of books under the other end to form an incline. Test each object several times, putting it in different places on the "slide."

Example

Friction on a cardboard surface:

Object	Angle	Coefficients of friction F_s and F_k
A flat piece of sandstone	31°	0.6
A flat piece of hard driftwood	22°	0.4
Twenty-five cent coin	12°	0.2

In each case, the difference between F_s and F_k was too small to measure.

Unit 2

A Simpler Experiment with Friction for Younger Students

Materials

- Wooden board or piece of stiff cardboard with a uniform surface, approximately three feet long and one foot wide
- Selection of rather flat objects, such as pieces of wood, metal washers, coins, flat rocks, books, and so on. You can make some objects with very rough surfaces by gluing sandpaper onto them.

Experiment

When you set up a board at an angle and put an object on it, the object either stays where it is, or starts sliding. Measure the angle between the board and the surface of the table, and record the result. The picture shows one method for doing this. In it, the board is at a 30° angle.

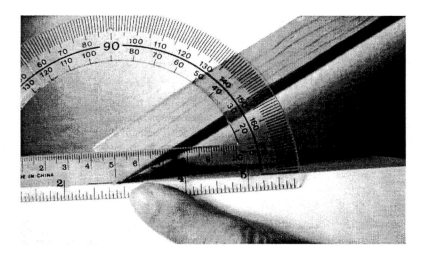

Repeat this several times until you find a critical angle, namely, the angle such that the object slides if the board is even a little steeper, and stays where it is when the board is flatter.

Example of a card on which data are recorded:

Object: Piece of smooth soft wood Ramp: Wooden (poplar) board		
	Results	
Angle in degrees	Stay	Slide
30°	X	
35°	X	
45°		X
40°		X
33°	X	
34°		X
35°		X
34°		X
36°		X
34°	X	
33°	X	
The critical angle is 34.5° (with an error of approximately 0.5°).		

Unit 3

Getting a Grip on Friction

Here are some questions that one can answer through an experiment.

1. Does the amount of surface area of an object that is in contact with the surface the object is sitting on affect the coefficient of friction?
2. Does the weight of the object that is in contact with a surface influence the coefficient of friction?
3. If I change the surface from poplar wood to fine-grained sandpaper, how does this affect the coefficient of friction?
4. Another question is whether the center of gravity of an object affects its coefficient of friction, namely, if the center of gravity is "farther down" the ramp, will the object start to slide at a lower angle?
5. You might think that if you put a quarter on a horizontal poplar board and raise the board, the quarter will begin to slide at some angle A. If you first raise the board to an angle, and then put the quarter on it, the quarter will slide at an angle lower than A. So the question is, what is going on here?

Can you collect data to try to answer one of the questions above?

Experiment 1

Does the amount of surface area of the object that is in contact with the surface affect the coefficient of friction?

The mathematical model for the coefficient of static friction, F_s, states that F_s is equal to the tangent of the ramp angle at which the object still stays in place (any increase in the angle will cause the object to slide). Note that surface area is not included in the mathematical model for the coefficient of friction. Does this hold in reality?

I took a block consisting of 4 cubic inches. Its weight was 46 grams.

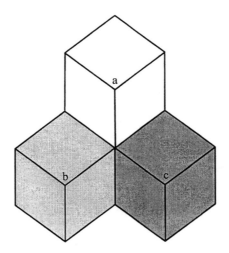

With the three "points" (vertices) marked a, b, and c in the figure touching a poplar ramp at angle 14.5°, the block just begins to slide. (I took several measurements of this.) The block looks like this:

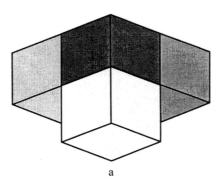

tan (14.5°) = 0.26

With three square inches of the block touching the ramp (so it is sitting as shown in the first figure), the block just begins to slide at 14.0°. (Again, I took several measurements.)

tan (14°) = 0.25

I attached a string to the block and attached the string to a spring scale. When I pulled the block horizontally with the spring scale along the poplar wood, the scale read 10 grams.

10 / 46 = 0.22, which is very close to 0.25 and 0.26

I want to collect a few more pieces of data (e.g., what happens when a block made of four cubic inches has 4 square inches that touch the surface?), but thus far it appears that surface area influences the coefficient of friction very little.

Experiment 2

Does the weight of the object influence the coefficient of friction? (Note that the weight of the object is not included in the math model for the coefficient of friction!)

I put a quarter on the poplar board as the board lay horizontally. I raised the board slightly, tapping it underneath. The quarter began to slide when the ramp reached an angle of 17°. So the coefficient of friction is tan 17° = 0.305.

I then put a small piece of scotch tape on the top of the quarter and taped a second quarter onto the first one. The two quarters began to slide at about 16.5°. So the coefficient of friction is about 0.296. Now I make a stack of five quarters, with the same original side down. This time the quarters started to slide (with a little tapping) at about 16°. So the coefficient of friction is approximately:

tan (16°) = 0.287

I want to collect more data, but I can say that the coefficient of friction does not appear to depend on the weight of the object.

Experiment 3

What effect does finely grained sandpaper have on the coefficient of friction of quarters?
I repeated Experiment 2, but I taped sandpaper onto my ramp. Here are my data:

> One quarter begins to slide at 34°. Coefficient of friction = tan (34°) = 0.67
> Two quarters begin to slide at 36°. Coefficient of friction = tan (36°) = 0.73
> Five quarters begin to slide at 39°. Coefficient of friction = tan (39°) = 0.81

Here my data show definitely that sandpaper makes the coefficient of friction for quarters go way up (by a factor of two or three!). But does weight influence the coefficient of friction for quarters on sandpaper? From the three numbers I have, I am not sure.

Does the center of gravity (the way the object is put on the ramp) influence the coefficient of friction? According to the math model, it should not. (But if the object's center of gravity is too high, the object may topple rather than slide!)

Why does it seem that an object put on a horizontal board must be raised to a higher angle before it begins to slide, than the same object placed on a board already at an angle?

In the first case, static friction must be overcome in order for the object to move. (Static friction is greater than or equal to kinetic friction.)

In the second case, static friction does not have to be overcome; the object is never stationary; it is always moving.

Here is another question a student asked: What is the difference between friction and inertia?

Friction is a force (it is measured in newtons). Forces are vectors. Any force is a relationship between two objects. When we talk about a force acting on an object, we describe the net effect of all such relationships.

Inertia is an informal name for the property of matter that says that whenever one observes an acceleration (a change of velocity), there are some forces present. These forces change the velocity of the observed object, or they change the velocity of the observer, or they do both. The technical term that describes the "amount of inertia" is mass (it is measured in kilograms). Mass is a scalar; it has only a magnitude and no direction. The mass of an object is a property of the object itself and doesn't depend on its relation to other objects.

The important fact is that acceleration depends only on the strength of the force and the mass of the object, and not on the kind of force that is acting (e.g., gravity, friction, magnetic attraction, and so on). We can imagine an object that could be quite heavy to lift but that could be easily pulled by a magnetic force. But no such object exists.

Chapter 5

Pulleys and Ramps

Unit 1

Pulleys

Setting

Working with pulleys requires that they hang down from some structure. The best setting is to have a stand that is two or more feet tall on each table. The stand has a horizontal bar that can be moved up and down, and movable hooks for attaching a string or pulleys.

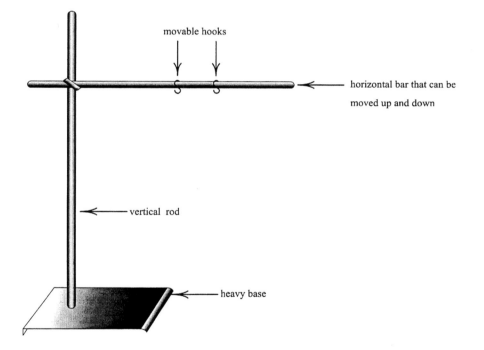

But you can improvise. For example:

- With strong tape, attach a stick to the side of a table, so that the stick is horizontal, and hang the pulleys or strings from the stick. But then you have to sit on the floor to do the measurements.
- Or let one person simulate the stand, holding a pulley or a string in one hand and holding his/her wrist with the other hand to keep it steady.
- Or tie a string to the girders in the ceiling, and tie the pulley onto the string. (This is the option that we chose, and it was quite acceptable.)

Other Equipment (One Set Per Table)

- one pulley
- two or more reasonably heavy iron nuts or other such objects that are easy to handle
- one spring scale
- one pressure scale
- string that is flexible and thin but strong
- calculators

Experiment 1

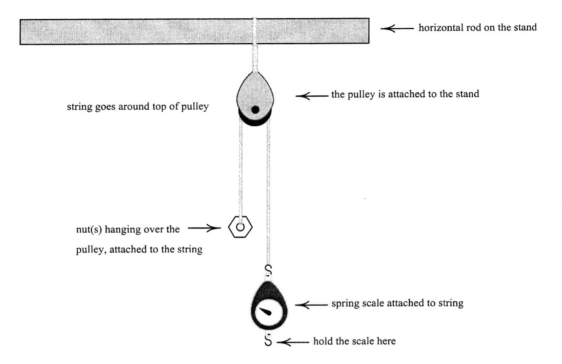

horizontal rod on the stand

the pulley is attached to the stand

string goes around top of pulley

nut(s) hanging over the pulley, attached to the string

spring scale attached to string

hold the scale here

Weigh the nut(s) on the pressure scale. Hang them over the wheel of the pulley as shown.
1. Attach the pulley to the horizontal rod on the stand.
2. Attach the weighs to the string.
3. Put the string around the top of the pulley.
4. Attach the scale to the other end of the string.

Read the spring scale. Record the weight of the nut and the force (from the spring scale) in newtons. They should be the same.

Experiment 2

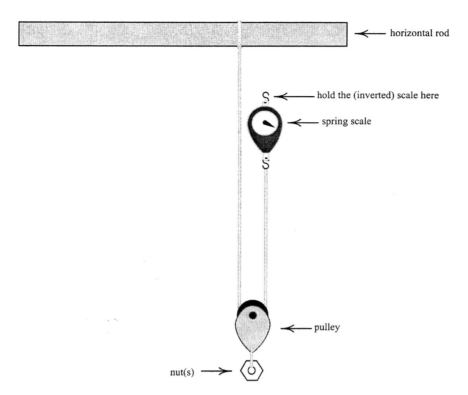

Weigh the pulley and nut(s) together on the pressure scale. Hang the nut(s) and pulley as shown.

1. Attach the nuts to the pulley.
2. Attach the string to the stand.
3. Put the string around the top of the pulley.
4. Attach to the other end of the string.

Record the weight and the force (from the spring scale) in newtons. The force should be half of the weight.

Explanation

In both experiments, we have a stable arrangement. Therefore, the forces acting on both ends of the string threaded around the wheel of the pulley are the same. So in the first experiment, the force recorded on the spring scale is equal to the weight of the nut(s). In the second experiment, the weight of the pulley and nut(s) is equally distributed between the spring scale and the hook on the horizontal rod. So the scale records only half of their weight.

Remark

1. A pulley and a system of connected pulleys are examples of "simple machines," which were used long before the modern industrial era.

Unit 2

Holding Objects on Ramps

Introduction

In these problems, students must convert and record forces in newtons. This is not just an exercise in conversions! A reminder:

- one kilogram (of weight)   = 2.2 lb (approximately)
  = 9.81 newtons
  = $9.81 * 10^5$ dynes

- one ounce = 28.4 grams (approximately)
- one pound = 4.46 newtons (one newton is about 3.6 oz)

1. When students start studying dynamics, most of the forces they study are not due to gravity, so using grams (of weight) and ounces loses its intuitive appeal.
2. In many formulas, both mass and force occur simultaneously, and using grams (of force) and grams (of mass) in the same formula leads to utter confusion. Thus, students should get accustomed to measuring forces in newtons (and in dynes, when appropriate) when they start learning dynamics.

Ramps

Building a Ramp

For this lesson ramps can be made from the back covers of 8½ by 11 inch yellow pads. Score two lines one inch from the edges and bend the sides up. This prevents the cardboard from bending.

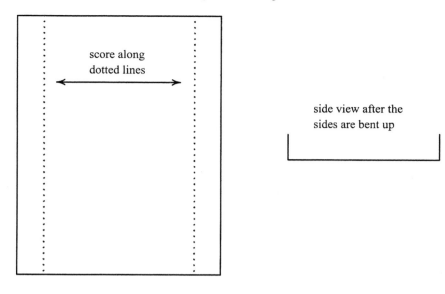

Attach one side of the ramp to the table with tape. Support the other end with a stack of books or other heavy objects.

Side view

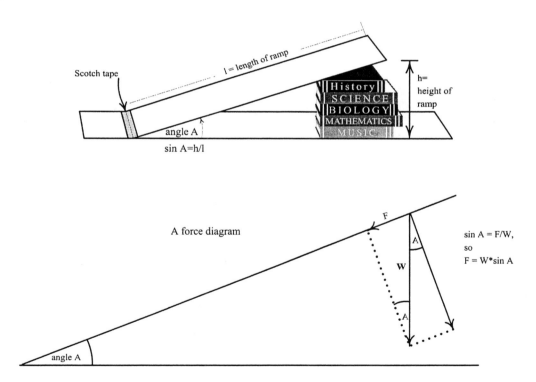

Preparing an Object to Be Held on the Ramp

Using tape, fasten a heavy nut or a rock to the top of a toy truck. Weigh it on the pressure scale and tie it with a thin string to a spring scale.

Measurements

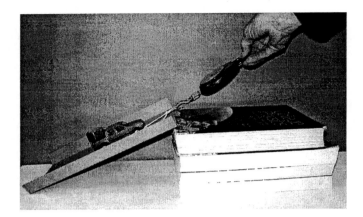

Vary the angle A between the ramp and the table. For each position, measure sin A. Put the toy car on the ramp and hold it in place with the spring scale that is put above it on the ramp. Measure the force that is recorded on the scale.

Remark

Students should measure sin A in two ways:
  a) Measure angle A with a protractor and compute sin A with a scientific calculator.
  b) Measure the length l of the ramp and the height h of the back of the ramp above the table, and compute (with a calculator) sin A = h/l.

Students record the data as follows (see some sample data in the table on the next page):

Weight W of the car with its load (in newtons).
Force F recorded on the spring scale (in newtons).

Angle A	sin A	F	W * sin A

Theoretical Predictions

The last two columns, F and W * (sin A), should be approximately equal. The force of weight W, acting straight down, can be decomposed into two perpendicular components:
  • One that acts parallel to the ramp (downward, but not vertically) with strength W * (sin A).
  • The other that presses on the ramp in a direction perpendicular to its slope with strength W * (cos A).

We measure with the spring scale only the first force, parallel to the ramp, so we expect that
        F = W * (sin A).

We can compute the second force, w * cos A, perpendicular to the ramp, when we know F:

tan A = sin A / cos A
cos A = sin A / tan A
W * cos A = w * sin A / tan A
W * cos A = F / tan A

History

Ramps were one of the "simple machines" that were known in antiquity. Pulling an object on a ramp requires less force than hauling it straight up. So, ramps were often used in many construction projects. Mathematical problems concerning ramps are known from cuneiform tablets from the Middle East dated around 2000 B.C.

Data from My Experiment

Weight (W) of the car with a load, in newtons: W = 1.3 newtons						
Angle (A)	Height (h) of ramp	Length (l) of ramp	h / l	sin A from scientific calculator	Force (F) recorded on spring scale (in newtons)	F = W * (sin A)
22°	4 inches	11 in.	0.36	0.37	0.45 newtons	0.48
30°	5.5 inches	11 in.	0.50	0.50	0.60 newtons	0.65
40°	7.5 inches	11 in.	0.68	0.64	0.70 newtons	0.83
70°	10 inches	11 in.	0.91	0.94	1.20 newtons	1.22

Unit 3

Pulling and Holding Objects on Ramps and Lifting Objects Up

Materials

- a few objects with weights that can be measured with reasonable accuracy on a spring scale (not too light)
- some small carts with wheels that you can use to pull the objects
- spring scale
- wooden boards 2–3 feet long to act as ramps
- string

Question

What are the forces that are needed to hold an object on a ramp and to pull an object up the ramp?

Experiments

Pull objects up the ramp or hold them still. Measure and record the forces involved and other "relevant" variables.

The variables we consider are:
- w   the weight of the object
- f   the pulling (holding) force that acts along the ramp
- A   the angle of incline of the ramp
- the contact of the object with the ramp (either dragging, or on wheels). (This can be described by a coefficient of static friction, F_s, and a coefficient of kinetic friction, F_k, which remain unknown in the experiments described below.)

Remarks

1. If the object is pulled on a cart, its weight is the sum of the weight of the object and the weight of the cart.
2. When you pull the object, pull it very slowly with a constant speed. Let one person pull the object and another person read the scale.
3. Tie a short string to the object and hook the scale to the string. When you pull or hold the scale, keep it parallel to the ramp.

An Example of a Written Record

Object ID: _____
Weight in newtons: _____
Ramp's angle in degrees: _____
Holding force in newtons: _____
Pulling force in newtons: _____

Theory

Holding an Object on a Ramp

The force f (directed up the ramp) that holds an object must be such that:
$$w * (\sin A) - F_s * w * (\cos A) \le f \le w * (\sin A) + F_s * w * (\cos A)$$

Because $w * (\sin A)$ is the component of weight pulling the object down the ramp and $F_s * w * (\cos A)$ is the static friction helping to keep the object in place.

When $F_s * w * (\cos A) > w * (\sin A)$, then f can be negative (so f pushes the object downward). (Or the object just sits on the ramp.)
When $f > w * (\sin A) + F_s * w * (\cos A)$, the object starts moving up the ramp.

Pulling an Object up the Ramp

The force pulling the object up the ramp with a constant speed is
$$f = w*(\sin A) + Fk * w * (\cos A).$$

The force f equals the component of weight pulling the object down, plus the friction resisting the movement. A bigger f would accelerate the object. For a smaller f, the object will slow down until it stops.

Remark

1. Pushing an object requires the same force as pulling it.

The Work That Is Done

Let L be the length of the ramp and H be the height of its top above its bottom. The relationship between these variables is:

$$H / L = \sin A$$

The work of lifting the object to height H, which we call W_l, is:

$$W_l = H * w$$

(w is the weight of the object.)
The force required is w.

The work of pulling it along the ramp, which we call W_p, is:

$$W_p = L * f$$

The force required is f.

But $L = H / (\sin A)$, and $f = w * (\sin A) + F_d * w * (\cos A)$ (from above) (a component due to gravity plus a component due to friction. Therefore:

$$
\begin{aligned}
W_p = L * f &= (H / \sin A) * f = (H / \sin A) * [w * (\sin A) + F_k * w * (\cos A)] \\
&= H * w + (H / \sin A) * F_k * w * (\cos A) \\
&= H * w + F_k * L * w * (\cos A) \text{ (substituting L for H / sin A)} \\
&= W_l + F_k * L * w * (\cos A)
\end{aligned}
$$

(The work of "lifting" plus the work needed due to friction; the first one is proportional to the height H, and the second one to the length L of the ramp.)

What does this mean?
1. Using a ramp usually allows you to do the work with less force because $f = w * (\sin A) + F_k * w * (\cos A) < w$, if we use wheels, or if we provide a small coefficient of friction F_k by some other means.
2. But the total work is *never* smaller when you pull an object up a ramp to a height H rather than lifting it to the same height.

The best case (when there is no friction) yields $W_p = W_l$. In most practical cases $W_p > W_l$, so we have a tradeoff, namely, less force but more work.

Unit 4

Spring-Powered Cars

Materials

For this lesson you need:
- spring-powered toy cars
- a ramp (whose angle can be adjusted)
- good scales
- protractors
- scientific calculators

Students work in groups, sitting around tables. Each group must have a set of supplies and at least one car.

Question

What is the force exerted by the coiled spring?

Solution

Find the smallest angle A of the ramp such that the car (when it is spring-loaded) cannot drive uphill on the ramp. For this angle, the component of the weight w of the car parallel to the ramp is equal in magnitude to the force f exerted by the spring. Therefore, $f = w * (\sin A)$.

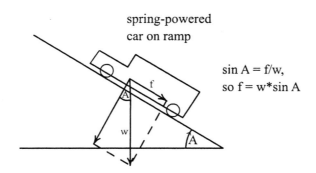

spring-powered
car on ramp

$\sin A = f/w$,
so $f = w * \sin A$

Procedure

1. Weigh the car in grams (of weight). Record it in grams (g).
2. Experiment until you find the smallest angle A such that the car cannot go up the ramp when it is spring loaded. Record all your attempts (the angles you try, and the outcomes—whether or not the car can go up the ramp).
3. For the smallest angle such that the car cannot go up the ramp, compute the force f, and convert the car's weight in grams to newtons. (One kilogram = 9.81 newtons, so one gram = 0.00981 newton.) Record the answer in newtons.

Some Sample Data

My car weighs w = 101 grams ≈ 1 newton. I spring loaded the car and I experimented. The smallest angle A of the ramp such that the car cannot drive uphill on the ramp is 12°. So, the force f exerted by the coiled spring is w * sin (12°) = 1 * 0.208 ≈ 0.21 newton. Since one newton is about 3.6 ounces, the force exerted by the car's spring is about ¾ ounce.

Pictures of coiled springs inside an old-fashioned clock and a toy car are in chapter 8, unit 3, Potential Energy.

Chapter 6

Moving Objects

Unit 1

Racing Cars

Question

Some of us discovered that the spring coil in one of the two cars we were testing gave a lot more force (when measured on the ramp) than the one in the other car. So some of us raced the two cars on a horizontal surface and discovered that indeed the car with more force actually out-raced the other one! Is there a formula to predict, from force data on a ramp, how much better one car will race than another? Can you predict the distance or the speed?

Answer

If we ignore friction (which is a reasonable first approximation), and if we assume that the force is approximately constant until the spring unwinds, we have
$$M(t) = force * t$$
where $M(t)$ is the momentum at time t from the start.

But
$$M(t) = v(t) * mass, \text{ so } v(t) = (force / mass) * t$$
where $v(t)$ is the speed at time t.

After the spring unwinds at time t_0, the car will travel with a constant speed $v(t_0)$. (But then the friction that we have ignored starts playing the main role.)

The distance d that is traveled in the time t that passes until the spring unwinds is
$$d = [v(t) / 2] * t = [(force * t) / (2 * mass)] * t$$
because $v(t) / 2$ is the average speed during time t.

We rewrite this as:
d = (t2/2) * (force/mass)

Thus, solving for t, we have:
    t = √(2 * d * mass / force)

Therefore, for short races, the car with the better (smaller) mass/force ratio will win.

Let's consider only "drag races" that are short enough that the springs of the cars don't unwind completely.

Let car 1 have mass m_1, and let it exert a force f_1, and let car 2 have mass m_2, and let it exert a force f_2. Let d be the distance. And let the units of measurement be mass in kilograms, distance in meters, force in newtons, and time in seconds.

Then, the first car travels distance d in √(2 * d * m_1 / f_1) seconds, and the second one travels distance d in √(2 * d * m_2 / f_2) seconds.

Students may try to check these predictions experimentally. Because measurements of time will not be precise, the average of several races should be compared.

Unit 2

Instant Velocity

If the velocity of an object is constant (meaning that neither its magnitude v nor its direction changes), then during time t the object travels a distance d = v * t along a straight line. If the object changes its velocity, then the magnitude, a, of its acceleration (that is, its change of velocity) is proportional to the sum f of all the forces that act on the object and inversely proportional to its mass, m; a = f/m.

In everyday situations, the velocity of an object is rarely constant, but it usually changes rather slowly because the forces we encounter (with the exception of accidents) are rather weak.

To discuss changing velocities, we introduce the concept of "instant" velocity at a moment t0. In order to do so, we choose a value h that is small enough so that within time h the velocity remains (practically) constant.

Then we look at the position of the object at the moments $t_0 - h/2$ and $t_0 + h/2$.

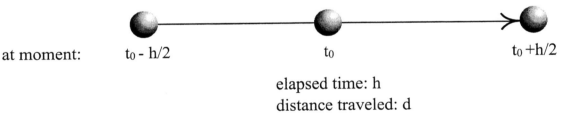

at moment: $t_0 - h/2$ t_0 $t_0 + h/2$

elapsed time: h
distance traveled: d

Now we take v = d/h as the magnitude of the instant velocity at the moment t0, and the direction from the beginning location to the end location of the object as the direction of instant velocity.

So, for example, if h = 0.01 s and d = 10 cm, then at the time t0 the object is moving with a speed of v = 10 m/s in the direction indicated by the arrow.

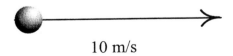

10 m/s

There are many ways to measure or compute instant velocity. For example, police use a "radar gun" to measure and record the magnitude of the instant velocity of cars in order to catch speeders.

Unit 3

Measuring Average Speed

The principle for measuring average speed is simple. Measure the distance and the time traveled, and compute their quotient. But in classroom tasks this is not so simple because measuring brief periods of time with a stopwatch is a little tricky and not very precise.

Experiment 1

Measure the average speed of objects falling from heights of 0.5 m, 1 m, 1.5 m, and 2 m. Use small, rather dense, objects such as pebbles, marbles, small metal nuts, and so on. Measure the heights precisely. You may need to stand on a chair or table to drop an object from a height of two meters. Measure the time with a stopwatch. (You need at least two people to carry out the experiment.) Repeat the measurements several times and record all your results.

Compare your data to the data in the table below. This will give you an idea of the accuracy of your measurements, including any possible systematic errors.

Height in m	Time in s	Speed in m/s
0.5	0.32	1.6
1.0	0.45	2.2
1.5	0.55	2.7
2.0	0.64	3.1

In order to observe speeds that are easier to measure, it is better to study objects that are rolling or sliding on a ramp. When the ramp is not too steep, objects move much more slowly than an object that is falling, and the time of movement is easier to measure. This is a procedure that was used by Galileo Galilei (1564–1642) when he did his experiments. The story that he dropped objects from the tower of Pisa is possible, but it is probably false. It would be quite dangerous for people who were walking below!

Experiment 2

Roll a selection of toy cars down a ramp. Carefully measure the distance they travel, the angle of incline of the ramp, the weight of the cars, and the time of travel. Prepare a table of data containing all the measured quantities and the (average) speed of the rolling car, computed as distance/time.

What do you observe?

Remarks

1. At least two people are needed to carry out the experiment. One person measures the time and the other holds the car. It is useful to put an index card in a vertical position at the end of the ramp. The car will hit the card when it reaches the bottom. This will help you get a more accurate measure of the time of travel. You measure the distance from the front of the car to the bottom of the ramp.

   The goal of these two experiments is just to observe what happens and to get practice in measuring average speed. It is preliminary to a discussion and explanation of what happens in terms of forces and momentums.

2. Using cars is better than rolling balls because the movement of a ball consists of two parts—going down the ramp and spinning. But in a car, the spinning wheels are small and light, so only the movement downward needs to be taken into consideration. You may slide other objects, such as coins, down the ramp, but then friction starts playing a central role.

Speed at One Moment of Time

The speed of a moving object may vary in time. So besides the concept of average speed over a period of time, we have the concept of speed at an instant moment. We only approximate it by taking averages over very small periods of time, or we compute it from other measurements. We usually write speed at a moment t as $v(t)$, and read it, "v of t."

What happens when a car is rolling down a ramp?

The weight of the car is $w = g * m$, where m is its mass and $g = 9.81$ m/s/s. It is directed downward. On a ramp slanted by A degrees, the component of weight parallel to the ramp is the force:
$$f = w * (\sin A) = g * m * (\sin A)$$

At the beginning, for time $t = 0$, the momentum, $M(0)$, of the car is
$$M(0) = 0,$$
because $M(0) = m * v(0)$ and $v(0) = 0$ (the car is still not moving).

Under the influence of the force f, the momentum is increasing, and after time t it is
$$M(t) = M(0) + f * t.$$

But $M(t) = m * v(t)$, so
$$m * v(t) = 0 + g * m * (\sin A) * t,$$
and, therefore,
$$v(t) = g * (\sin A) * t.$$

If the total time of travel is t1, then at the end, the car reaches the speed
$$v(t_1) = g * (\sin A) * t_1,$$
which has been increasing uniformly from the initial speed 0.

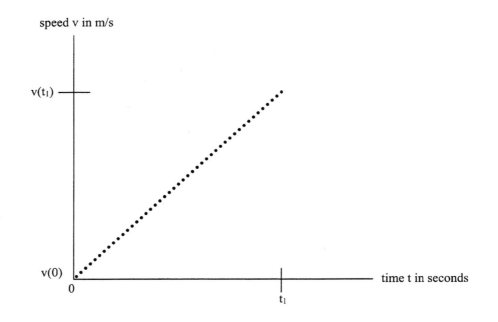

Thus the average speed is the mean of the initial and final speeds, namely:

$\text{av\_speed} = v(t_1) / 2 = g * (\sin A) * t_1 / 2$

We have already measured average speed before, so we can now check how well our measurements agree with our predictions. But we can get even more from this formula.

The distance traveled, d, is

$d = \text{av\_speed} * \text{time\_of\_travel}$
$\quad = \text{av\_speed} * t_1$
$\quad = g * (\sin A) * t_1 / 2 * t_1$
$\quad = g * (\sin A) * t_1^2 / 2,$

and, therefore,

$t_1 = \sqrt{[2 * d/(g * \sin A)]}.$

Thus, we can predict the time it takes to move down the ramp simply from the distance of travel and the angle of incline. But even the best car is slightly slowed down by friction, so the values that are predicted may be a little different from what we observed, even if we make precise measurements.

When the ramp is vertical, $A = 90°$, and $\sin A = 1$, and the body is just free falling. So the time of free fall from a height h, if we ignore air drag, is:

$t_1 = \sqrt{(2 * h/g)}$

Unit 4

Rolling Balls

The Experimental Setting

Using strong packaging tape, attach to a desk or to a smooth wooden board (approximately 3 feet long) two yardsticks or meter sticks, or two straight, smooth pieces of wood, forming a corridor. The width of the corridor should be slightly wider than the diameter of the balls you are using, but not much wider.

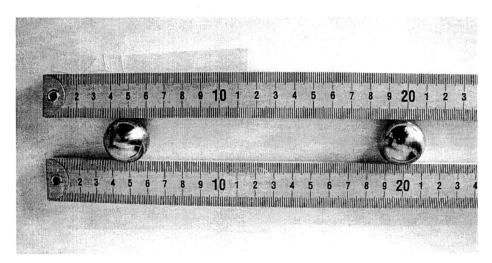

The balls can be marbles, ball bearings, or golf balls, but not ping pong balls.

Each group of four students should have one such setting.

Experiments

The experiments deal with the collision of two or more balls. Students perform experiments and carefully describe in writing what they did and what the results were. There are no precise measurements, but students should use some qualitative scale of the speed of the balls (slow, fast, very fast). (When a ball stops in the corridor, its position can be recorded precisely.)
Each experimental condition should be repeated several times.

Examples of Observations

1. A slow ball hits an identical stationary ball.

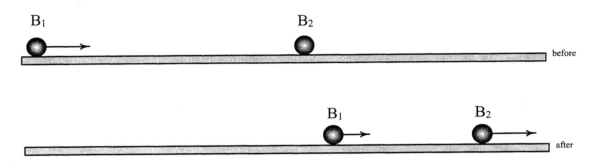

When a slowly rolling ball hits a stationary ball, the stationary ball rolls slowly, and the hitting ball follows it very slowly.

2. A fast ball hits an identical stationary ball.

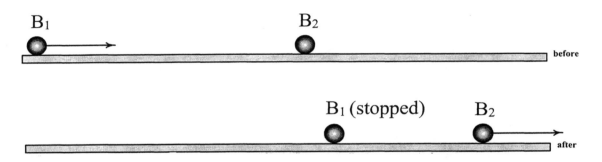

When a fast-rolling ball hits a ball, the ball that is hit rolls fast and the hitting ball stops a few inches from the collision spot.

3. A fast ball hits two identical balls.

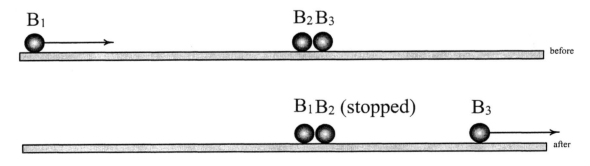

When a fast-rolling ball hits two balls, one ball rolls fast, and two balls stay in the initial position.

After students become familiar with the phenomena, the dynamics of collisions between balls should be discussed. Students should learn the concepts involved (some of them may be new to them), the units of measurement, and relevant formulas. Some reading material should be assigned.

Comparing the results of the experiments with theoretical predictions, students will see that the match is not perfect because theoretical formulas are derived with the assumption that collisions are perfectly elastic, there is no friction, and so on.

Finally, students may design an additional experiment or repeat one they have previously done, trying to make a prediction about the results and justifying their prediction on the basis of their new knowledge.

Unit 5

Sliding Balls

When a ball rolls, its movement consists of two motions that occur simultaneously—sliding and spinning.

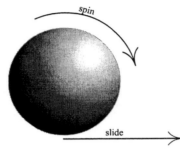

The "equator" of the spinning ball moves the fastest (with speed v1) and the "poles," which lie on the axis of rotation, remain stationary. Besides, different points on the surface and on the inside of the ball move in different directions.

In the sliding movement, all points of the ball move in the same direction with the same speed, v_2.

In usual situations $v_1 = v_2$ and the axis of rotation is parallel to the ground and perpendicular to the direction of movement. (Roll a ball slowly on a table to see what this means.)

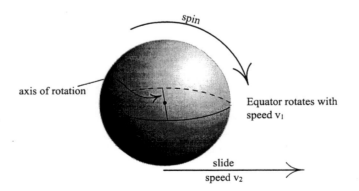

At any given time, the point at the top of the ball, P, moves with a speed of 2v; the center of the ball, Q, moves with a speed of v, which is called the speed of the ball; and the point that touches the ground has a speed of zero.

But a ball can move in many different ways depending on the surface, the speed, and the way the movement was initiated.

A skillful pool player can make a ball slide without any spin, or make it spin backward, or make it spin around a vertical axis. These are only a few of the things a skillful player can do.

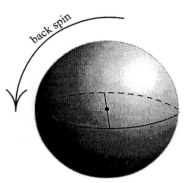

Many such unusual movements also occur also in everyday situations. When a ball is resting on a smooth surface and you hit it hard, it starts its motion by sliding; and only a few moments later, because of the friction between the ball and the ground, will the slide turn into a roll.

All these factors influence the outcomes of collisions, and this is the reason that playing pool well requires a lot of mental work.

Unit 6

Questions and Answers about Colliding Balls

1. Suppose I have a line of golf balls in a corridor. If I roll one golf ball into the line, all the ones except the one on the end stay still, and the one on the end moves. Why? If momentum equals mass times velocity, why don't two balls on the end move, but with half of the velocity of the original ball? Or three balls, with one-third the velocity?

2. When two balls collide, momentum is preserved. Is anything else preserved?

3. Suppose I have a lighter ball and a heavier ball of the same volume. If I roll the lighter ball into the heavier ball, the lighter ball goes backwards (quickly), and the heavier ball moves a little. What is happening? Compare this to (1) in which the rolled golf ball stops moving.

Answer to (2). When two balls collide, momentum is preserved. Is anything else preserved?

Dynamics deals with movements in the presence of forces. The two basic quantities that are preserved in an isolated system are:

momentum and *energy*

Changes in the amount and direction of momentum, and changes in the amount of energy of moving objects, are caused by forces. And conversely, any change of momentum or energy manifests itself as a force. As long as we restrict our discussion only to momentum, we have a very incomplete picture of what happens.

A more complete picture for colliding balls is rather complex, because there are two kinds of momentum, linear, M_l, which is due to movement along some trajectory, and rotational, M_r, related to spin.

There are also two kinds of kinetic energy which play a role in a collision.
Again, one is connected to linear motion, Ek_l, and the other is connected to rotation, Ek_r.

	Rotational	Linear
Momentum	M_r	$M_l = m * v$
Kinetic energy	Ek_r	$Ek_l = m*v^2 / 2$

Here, m is the mass of an object and v is its speed. We have not looked at any formulas dealing with M_r and Ek_r.

Without friction, linear and rotational quantities can be studied separately. But even a small amount of friction allows the transfer of one kind of momentum or energy into the other.

At present we will ignore rotational quantities, and this will allow us to explain some phenomena, but not all of them.

The two preservation rules are:
1. The sum of the momentums (as vectors) before an elastic collision is the same as the sum of the momentums after an elastic collision.
2. The sum of the kinetic energies before an elastic collision is the same as the sum of the kinetic energies after an elastic collision.

(With golf balls, marbles, etc., you observe collisions that are almost elastic. A collision of two wet clay balls is not elastic.)

Answer to (1). Suppose I have a line of golf balls in a corridor. If I roll one golf ball into the line, all the ones except the one on the end stay still, and the one on the end moves. Why? If momentum = mass * velocity, why don't two balls on the end move, but with half of the velocity of the original ball? Or three balls, with one-third the velocity?

Let's look at two balls, B_1 and B_2, and ignore any rotation.

Before the collision, ball B_1 is moving, and ball B_2 is not moving:

B_1 B_2

Before the collision:

ball	mass	velocity	momentum	kinetic energy (linear)
B_1	m	v	m * v	$M * v^2 / 2$
B_2	m	0	0	0

(Velocity that is directed to the right is positive, and velocity to the left is negative.)

What happens after the collision? Here v_1 and v_2 are the velocities of the two balls B_1 and B_2.

$m * v_1 + m * v_2 = m * v$, so $v_1 + v_2 = v$ (canceling m),
$m * v_1^2 / 2 + m * v_2^2 / 2 = m * v^2 / 2$, so $v_1^2 + v_2^2 = v^2$ (canceling m).
(This is preservation of momentum and preservation of energy.)

Let's solve the system of two equations (in v_1 and v_2):
$v_1 + v_2 = v$
$v_12 + v_22 = v^2$

$(v_1 + v_2)^2 - (v_1{}^2 + v_2{}^2) = (v_1{}^2 + 2v_1v_2 + v_2{}^2) - (v_1{}^2 + v_2{}^2) = 2 * v_1 * v_2,$
but also, since $v_1 + v_2 = v,$ and $v_1{}^2 + v_2{}^2 = v^2,$
$(v_1 + v_2)^2 - (v_1{}^2 + v_2{}^2) = v^2 - v^2 = 0.$
Therefore,
$\quad\quad$ either $\quad v_1 = 0,$ and $v_2 = v,$
$\quad\quad$ or $\quad\quad v_1 = v,$ and $v_2 = 0.$

But after the collision, the ball that is behind cannot be going faster than the ball in front, so $v_1 \leq v_2$. So the solution is, the first ball B_1 stops, and the other one, B_2, moves.

The situation after the collision:

$\quad\quad\quad\quad\quad\quad$ B₁ $\quad\quad\quad\quad\quad\quad\quad\quad\quad\quad\quad\quad\quad$ B₂

A chain of many balls can be viewed as a chain of collisions: the first ball hits the second; the second hits the third, and so on.

$\quad\quad\quad\quad\quad\quad$ B₁ $\quad\quad\quad\quad\quad\quad\quad\quad\quad\quad\quad\quad$ B₂ B₃ B₄

But in the presence of friction, which mixes forward movement with rotation, two balls can behave differently. However, three or more balls act as if rotation were not present!

Answer to (3). The question is, suppose I have a lighter ball and a heavier ball of the same volume. If I roll the lighter ball into the heavier ball, the lighter ball goes backwards (quickly), and the heavier ball moves a little. What is happening?

Work exactly as with question (1), using two different masses, m_1 and m_2, with $m_1 < m_2$, for B_1 and B_2, and using velocity v of the first ball, B_1, before the collision. All three of these, m_1, m_2, and v, are given. We want to know v_1 and v_2, the velocities of B_1 and B_2 after the collision.
Solve the system of equations:
$\quad\quad\quad m_1 * v_1 + m_2 * v_2 = m_1 * v \quad\quad\quad\quad$ preservation of momentum
$\quad\quad\quad m_1 * v_1{}^2 + m_2 * v_2{}^2 = m_1 * v^2 \quad\quad\quad$ preservation of kinetic energy

It has two solutions. One is $v_1 = v, v_2 = 0$. The other is the situation after the collision, when: $v_1 \leq v_2$

Remark

1. Either work algebraically (as shown in the example below), or reduce the two equations to one, and use SOLVER on the TI-83 Plus calculator to get numerical answers for specific data.

A worked-out example when the two masses, m_1 and m_2, are different:

Before the collision				
ball	mass	velocity	momentum	kinetic energy
B_1	m_1	v	m_1v	$m_1(v)^2 / 2$
B_2	m_2	0	0	0
After the collision				
ball	mass	velocity	momentum	kinetic energy
B_1	m_1	v_1	m_1v_1	$m_1(v_1)^2 / 2$
B_2	m_2	v_2	m_2v_2	$m_2(v_2)^2 / 2$

Since both momentum and kinetic energy are preserved, we know that
$$m_1v=m_1v_1 + m_2v_2$$
$$m_1v^2=m_1v_1^2 + m_2v_2^2$$

We know m_1, m_2, and v. For the purposes of this example, let's set $m_1 = 1$ and $m_2 = 3$. Then
(a) $\quad v =v_1 + 3 * v_2$
$\quad\quad v^2 = v_1^2 + 3v_2^2$

Then
$$(v_1 + 3 * v_2)^2 = v_1^2 + 3v_2^2$$
$$v_1^2 + 6v_1v_2 + 9v_2^2 = v_1^2 + 3v_2^2$$

So
$$6v_1v_2 + 6v_2^2 = 0$$
$$v_2(v_1 + v_2) = 0$$
So, either $v_2 = 0$, or $v_1 = -v_2$

So v_1, the velocity of B_1 after the collision, is equal to the velocity v_2 of B_2 after the collision, but in the opposite direction. But what exactly are the velocities v_1 and v_2?

(a) above gives
$$v = v_1 + 3 * v_2$$
Substituting $-v_2$ for v_1,
$$v = -v_2 + 3 * v_2$$
$$v = 2 * v_2, \text{ or}$$
$$v_2 = 0.5 * v$$

So after the collision, the ball in front, B_2, has a velocity v_2 equal to one half the velocity v that the ball behind, B_1, had before the collision.

Unit 7

Components of Velocity and Momentum

All directed quantities can be presented as sums of components.

Let's look at an object that has mass m = 130 kg, flying north, northeast (30° from vertical) in a straight line with a constant speed v of forty meters per second.

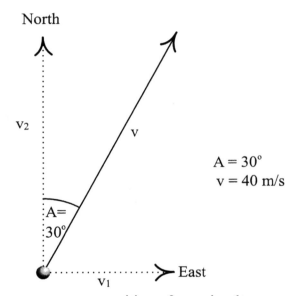

We may view its movement as a composition of two simultaneous motions:
straight east with speed $v_1 = v * (\sin A) = 20$ m/s, and
straight north with speed $v_2 = v *(\cos A) = 34.64$ m/s

Its momentum, M, has the same direction as its velocity, 30° north, northeast, and it has magnitude
$m * v = 5,200$ kg * m/s = 5.2 kg * km/s.

Because its momentum is a directed quantity, it also can be decomposed into two parts, with magnitudes M_1 and M_2:
straight east, $M_1 = M * (\sin A) = 2,600$ kg * m/s
straight north, $M_2 = M * (\cos A) = 5,503.3$ kg * m/s

But we should notice that:
$M_1 = M * (\sin A) = m * v * (\sin A) = m * v_1$
$M_2 = M * (\cos A) = m * v* (\cos A) = m * v_2$

Therefore, **the component of the momentum in a given direction is the product of its mass and of the component of its velocity in this direction.**

We should also notice that:

$$\sqrt{(M_1^2 + M_2^2)} = \sqrt{[M_2 * (\sin A)^2 + M_2 * (\cos A)^2]}$$
$$= M * \sqrt{[(\sin A)^2 + (\cos A)^2]}$$
$$= M.$$

Remark

1. Skill in handling algebraic and trigonometric expressions is very important in physics and other sciences. But it should not be considered a prerequisite. Learning rudiments of algebra in the context of science provides a concrete and meaningful environment to the otherwise abstract operations of algebra.

Unit 8

Momentum and Forces

A constant force f that acts on an object for a time t changes the *component* of the object's momentum, M_1, along the direction of the force. If the force and the component M_1 point in the same direction, M_1 increases; if they point in opposite directions, M_1 decreases. The amount of change (the difference in M_1), dM_1, is given by the following equation:

$$dM_1 = f * t$$

Here, distance is measured in meters, mass in kilograms, and force in newtons.

Therefore, the change is proportional to the magnitude of the force and the time it acts on the object.

Example

Consider an object of mass m = 2.5 kg that is moving up and to the right at a straight line inclined by A = 60° with respect to a horizontal line, with a speed v = 6 m/s.

Now consider a force f = 1.5 newtons that acts on the object along the horizontal line to the left for 2 seconds. What are the magnitude and direction of the object afterward?

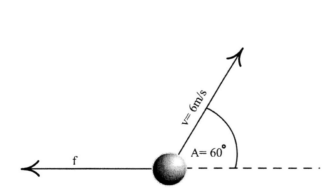

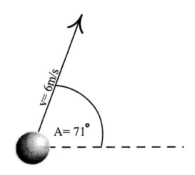

The object's momentum M in the direction of its movement is:

$$M = m * v = 2.5 * 6 \text{ kg} * \text{m/s} = 15 \text{ kg} * \text{m/s}$$

Its horizontal component, pointing to the right, is:

$$M_1 = M * (\cos A) = 15 \text{ kg} * \text{m/s} * (\cos 60°) = 7.5 \text{ kg} * \text{m/s}$$

Its vertical component, pointing up, is:

$$M_2 = M * (\sin A) = 15 \text{ kg} * \text{m/s} * (\sin 60°) = 13 \text{ kg} * \text{m/s}$$

Thus, the new component M1' is:

$$M_1' = M_1 - dM_1$$

where $dM_1 = f * t = 1.5 * 2$ newtons * sec = 3 (kg * m/s/s) * s = 3 kg * m/s.

So,

$$M1' = 7.5 - 3 \text{ kg * m/s} = 4.5 \text{ kg * m/s.}$$

The component M_2 remains unchanged.

Therefore the magnitude of the new momentum:

$$M' = \sqrt{(M_2' + M_2{}^2)} = 13.76 \text{ kg * m/s,}$$

so, its speed in the direction of movement is:

$$M'/m = 13.76 / 2.5 = 5.5 \text{ m/s.}$$

Its angle relative to the direction of the horizontal line is:

$$A' = \arctan (M_2/M_1) = 71°$$

Thus the object slowed down by 0.5 m/s (from 6 m/s to 5.5 m/s), and it changed its direction by 11° (from going up and to the right at an angle of 60°, to going up and to the right at an angle of 71°).

Unit 9

Preservation of Momentum

If you have a system of objects that do not interact (through forces) with their environment (or for which the interaction is so small that it can be ignored), then the sum of their momentums (which are directed quantities) remains the same.

If we have two or more hockey pucks colliding on ice, they form such a system. The force of gravity is cancelled by the pressure of the ice directed upward, and both air drag and friction are so small that they can be ignored.

Assume two hockey pucks have the same mass. If M_1 and M_2 are the momentums of the two pucks before a collision, and M_1' and M_2' are their momentums after the collision, then these sums before and after the collision, (as directed quantities, namely, as vectors), remain the same.

$$M_1 + M_2 = M_1' + M_2'$$

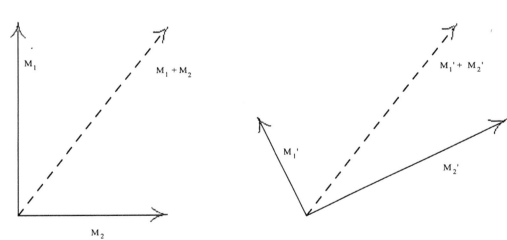

The actual directions and magnitudes of the new momentums depend on how the pucks collide, and therefore, they vary.

In many similar situations, what happens is much more complex. When we roll balls on a table, the force of gravity is neutralized by the table that supports the balls, and the friction of the rolling balls is minimal. But a rolling ball also has its rotational momentum, which in the presence of even very little friction can be transferred into (directional) momentum.

All pool players know that a ball's spin strongly influences what happens after a collision.

Remark

1. Basic physical interactions are usually simple, and they can be described by simple formulas. But they are difficult to observe in nature. This is the case because in most practical situations, so many factors interact that the role of each one, even when it is very simple, is difficult to see and to distinguish from the rest.

Unit 10

Momentum and Kinetic Energy

Problem

It is strange that a bullet weighing 0.004 kg (4 grams) and traveling at 600 m/s would have less momentum than a football player weighing 100 kilograms, who is walking at a speed of 2 m/s. It seems the bullet should have more momentum because it would do so much more damage. The bullet is much more difficult to stop. What is going on?

There are two concepts involved: kinetic energy, $m * v^2 / 2$, which is a scalar (it has just magnitude), and momentum, $m * v$, which is a vector (it has magnitude and direction). Energy can be measured in joules. One joule = one newton * meter.

	bullet	football player
kinetic energy = $m * v2/2$	720 joules	200 joules
momentum = m * v	2.4 kgm/s	200 kgm/s

So, we see that the bullet carries 720 / 200 = 3.6 times more kinetic energy than the football player. But the football player has 200 / 2.4 ≈83 times more momentum than the bullet.

The amount of damage, and how difficult it is to stop an object, depends on the object's kinetic energy and not on its momentum. In order to stop an object, a force f must act over a distance d, where
        kinetic energy = f * d.
Thus, a force of 100 newtons has to act over a distance of 2 meters to stop the football player. But the same force has to act over a distance of 7.2 meters to stop the bullet.

Momentum is related to the time that is needed to speed up an object, to slow it down, to change its direction, or to stop it. The relation between the time t needed by a force f to stop a moving object is

momentum = f * t

Thus, a force of 100 newtons requires a full 2 seconds to stop a heavy person (weighing 100 kilograms) who is moving relatively slowly (2 meters/second). But it requires only 0.024 seconds (24 milliseconds) to stop a light bullet (4 grams) that is moving fast (600 meters/second).

Chapter 7

Swinging Objects

Unit 1

Playing with Softballs Tied to a String

Materials

- very soft golf-sized balls made out of sponge
- string
- scissors
- a target

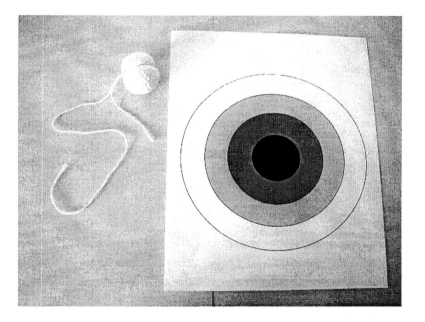

Task

Tie your sponge ball securely to a string. (One way to do this is to make a little cradle for it. But the balls we are using are very soft, so you may simply wrap a string tightly several times around the ball.) Extend the string out about a meter. Make a target on a chalkboard or on a piece of paper that you tape to a wall.

Your task is to swing the ball in a circle. While the ball is swinging, release the string and try to hit the target.

Question

When do you have to release the string in order to hit the target?

Try swinging the ball in circles of different orientations (horizontally, vertically, etc.) How do you have to adjust your release?

Can you explain what is happening?

Explanation

Suppose we swing the ball in a horizontal circle. The string constantly pulls the ball radially toward the center of the circle. Since the pull of the string is at all times perpendicular to the velocity of the ball, the force applied to the ball by the string continuously changes the direction of motion, but not its speed. (A force of this nature, which causes an object to move in a circle at constant speed, is called a centripetal force; the acceleration produced by a centripetal force is called centripetal acceleration.)

If the string is released, there is no more centripetal force, and therefore, no more centripetal acceleration. The ball no longer travels in a circle; it continues its motion in a straight line, tangent to the circle at the point where the ball was when the force was discontinued. So you need to release the string so that a straight line tangent to the circle at the point where the ball is goes through the target. (This does not take into account the force of gravity or air drag.)

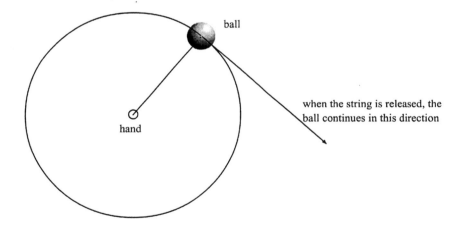

Unit 2

Swinging Weight

Introduction

In an experimental science course it is often necessary to give students formulas that are not derived or tested in class. Their task is then to understand the meaning of a given formula and to learn how to apply it in the problem at hand. The task below can be done on two different levels. It can be treated as a complex measurement task, in which some variables are controlled and measured, data are recorded, organized, and displayed, and only qualitative conclusions are derived. On a second level, experimental results are compared to theoretical predictions. The students must be familiar with the concept of force, and the formula to compute the centripetal force that is needed to keep an object in a circular orbit should be given to them without any special justification.

Materials

- assorted metal nuts or other small heavy objects that are easy to handle (you have to be able to tie them securely to a string)
- very strong string that is thin and flexible
- meter sticks and rulers
- stopwatches
- scientific calculators

Experiment

Make a hand-held pendulum by tying a nut very securely on a string and making a small loop on the other end to hold. Swing the nut in a circle above ground. By moving your hand, control the speed, and thereby make small circles or big ones. (Be careful not to hit anyone or anything else!)

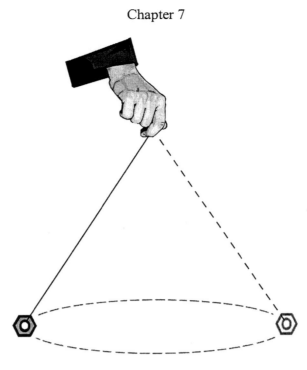

The rotating string "draws" a cone in space. The cone is flat and shorter when the nut moves fast, and it is narrow and taller when the nut slows down.

Measurements

Students work in groups of three. One swings the nut, and the other two make measurements.

First you measure the length, l, of the string from the point at which it is held to the center of mass of the nut; and you weigh the nut; call its weight w. Then one person keeps the time, t, with a stopwatch, and counts the number, n, of full rotations. The other person measures the diameter, d, (or the radius r = d / 2) of the circle the nut is moving around, using two meter sticks lying on the floor in a "cross" or X shape, overlapped at 50 cm. (This measurement is not very precise; it is an estimate.) The person who swings the nut should try to keep the size of the circle constant, and should try to keep his/her hand over the place where the two meter sticks intersect.

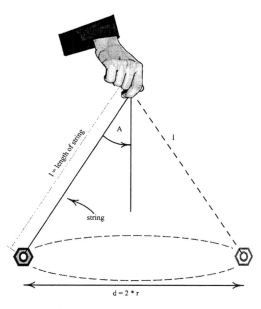

Values that are measured or computed and recorded:

- l   length of string in meters
- w   weight of nut in grams or kilograms
- $A = \arcsin(r/l)$ angle of the "cone" in degrees
- $T = t/n$ time of one rotation in seconds

Question

How does T depend on l, w, and A (which is controlled by hand movement)?

Theory

In order to make an object move around, we need to exert a force on the object toward the center (a centripetal force) that bends its trajectory into a circle. (In our experiment, this force is one component of the force that is exerted on the nut by the string held by a person's hand.) The object responds with an opposite force (a centrifugal force). (In our experiment this is the force that is exerted horizontally by the nut on the end of the string.)

The magnitude of the centrifugal (and centripetal) force fc is given by:

$$fc = m * r * q^2$$

Here, m is the mass of the object, r is the radius of the circle, and q is the angular speed of the object (the ratio of the angle traveled to the time of travel). If the mass is measured in kilograms, the radius in meters, and the angle in radians, then the centrifugal force, f_c, is measured in newtons.

About Radians

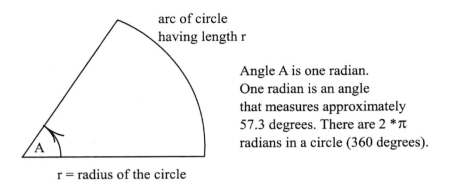

arc of circle
having length r

Angle A is one radian.
One radian is an angle
that measures approximately
57.3 degrees. There are 2 *π
radians in a circle (360 degrees).

r = radius of the circle

The speed v of the object along the circumference of the circle is:

$$v = r * q * t$$

Here, q is its angular velocity measured in radians. This is the reason for using radians in physics.

The Forces That Are Acting at the End of the String

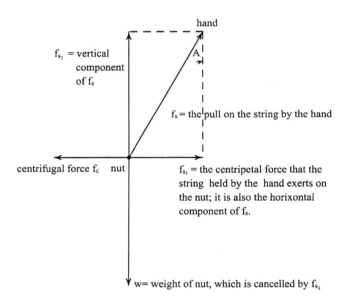

hand

f_{s_2} = vertical
component
of f_s

f_s = the pull on the string by the hand

centrifugal force f_c nut

f_{s_1} = the centripetal force that the
string held by the hand exerts on
the nut; it is also the horixontal
component of f_s.

w= weight of nut, which is cancelled by f_{s_2}

Centripetal Force

For an object to move along a curved path, a force must be applied to it. This force only changes the direction, not the speed, of the object and is called a *centripetal force*. Note that the direction of the force (and hence the acceleration) is *toward* the center of the curve. Centripetal means "center-seeking."

Centrifugal Force

The force that the nut exerts on the end of the string which is equal in strength but opposite in direction to the actual centripetal force. It is directed outward from the axis of rotation.

Relationships among the Magnitudes of Forces and Other Quantities

$f_{s1} = f_c$ and $f_{s2} = w$, but $f_{s1} / f_{s2} = \tan A$, and thus
$$f_c = w * (\tan A);$$
but $f_c = m * r * q^2$, where r is the radius of the circle, and q is the angular velocity of the nut, and $w = g * m$ where $g = 9.81$ m/s/s
So
$$m * r * q^2 = g * m * (\tan A)$$
and therefore,
$$q^2 = g * (\tan A)/r, \text{ so}$$
$$q = \surd\, [g * (\tan A)/r]$$

But $\sin A = r / 1$, and thus
the radius $r = 1 * \sin A$. And $\tan A = (\sin A) / (\cos A)$, and thus
$$q = \surd\, [g * (\tan A) / (1 * \sin A)]$$
$$q = \surd\, [g * (\sin A / \cos A) / (1 * \sin A)]$$
Sin A cancels, so
$$q = \surd\, [(g / \cos A) / 1]$$
Therefore,
$$q = \surd\, [g / (1 * \cos A)]$$
But T is the time of rotation, and
$$T = 2 * \pi / q, \text{ because } q = 2 * \pi / T$$
(i.e., q, which is angular speed, namely, angle divided by time, equals a whole rotation divided by the time of a whole rotation).
Thus,
$$T = (2 * \pi / \surd\, g) * \surd\, [1 * (\cos A)].$$
(g is the acceleration due to gravity, about 9.81 m/s^2.)
But notice that $\pi / \surd\, (9.81) = 1.00303 \approx 1$, so finally,
$$T = 2 * \surd\, [1 * (\cos A)]$$

This is the theoretical formula that predicts the results of the experiment. When the length, 1, is measured in meters, then T is given in seconds. So for $1 = 1$ m, and small angles, the period of one rotation is two seconds.

Remarks

1. The derivation may require additional algebraic steps. Show the steps separately in order to preserve the clarity of the main line of reasoning.
2. In order to get students familiar with the last formula, ask them to make a table for T as a function of l and A, for l = 0.5, 1, and 1.5 meters, varying A from 10 to 80 by 10 degrees, from 80 to 89 by 1 degree, and for 89 to 90 by 0.1 degree. (See the table at the end of the unit.)
3. You may use the TI-34 II calculator to generate the theoretical data T in the table at the end of the unit. We start with length l = 0.5 meters, and angle A = 10°, 20°, 30°, and so on.

Define

OP1 = √ [B * COS(ANS)]
Here B holds the string length l, and the value of angle A is stored in ANS.
Set DR to DEG, and FIX to 2.

To generate theoretical data, enter
0.5 →B ENTER
10 ENTER
OP1   rotation time T = 1.40 seconds
20 ENTER
OP1   rotation time T = 1.37 seconds
30 ENTER
OP1   rotation time T = 1.32 seconds

Sample data table for swinging weight. (To compute actual time, divide the number of full rotations by the time t.)

Angle A in degrees	Length of string = 0.5 meter		Length of string = 1 meter		Length of string = 1.5 meters	
	Actual time of one rotation	Theoretical time $T = 2 * \sqrt{(.5 * \cos A)}$	Actual time of one rotation	Theoretical time $T = 2 * \sqrt{(\cos A)}$	Actual time of one rotation	Theoretical time $T = 2 * \sqrt{(1.5 * \cos A)}$
10						
20						
30						

Chapter 8

Powered Flight

Unit 1

Playing with Units

Here is an activity to make some physical units come alive.

We have learned that weight is a force, and that one newton weighs about 3.6 ounces. Make a ball of clay that weighs 3.6 oz (about 98 grams). Hold it in your hand. You feel one newton of force.

Work is force * distance. One joule is one newton * meter. Mark a height of one meter on a wall. Lift your ball of clay from the floor up one meter. You have done one joule of work.

Power is work/second. One watt is one joule per second. Get a stopwatch. Again lift your ball of clay one meter, but do it in one second. You have demonstrated one watt of power.

Another unit of power is the horsepower. 1 horsepower = 746 watts. So, one way to demonstrate one horsepower of work is to lift 746 newtons one meter in one second. This is about 168 pounds.

Unit 2

Energy and Force

Force is related to momentum in the following way: An object changes its momentum from M_1 to M_2 in time t, if and only if the average, f, of the force that acts on this object during this period is:

$$f = (M_2 - M_1) / t$$

Force is also related to energy. An object changes its energy from E_1 to E_2 when it moves a distance d, if and only if the average f of the force acting on the object along the path of its movement is:

$$f = (E_2 - E_1)/d$$

This equation is often written as:

$$E_2 - E_1 = f * d$$

The product f * d, force times distance, is called work.

Example 1: A Ramp

The potential energy of an object due to the earth's gravity depends on how high up it is located.

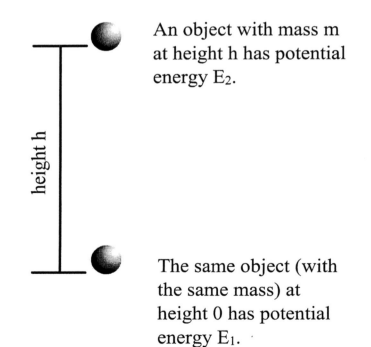

An object with mass m at height h has potential energy E_2.

height h

The same object (with the same mass) at height 0 has potential energy E_1.

We have: $E_2 - E_1 = g * m * h$

The difference in energy is measured in joules, the mass m is measured in kilograms, h in meters, and g = 9.81 m/s/s.

Now if we pull the object from level 0 to h along a ramp of length l without any measurable friction, then the force f required for pulling is:

$f = (E_2 - E_1)/l = g * m * h / l = g * m * (\sin A)$

Here, A is the angle of incline of the ramp (sin A = h / l).

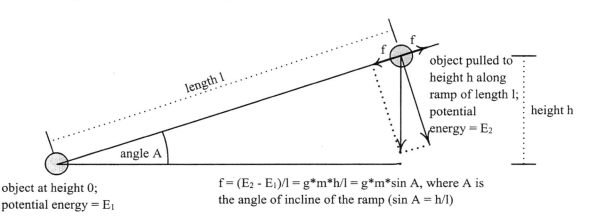

length l

f

f

object pulled to
height h along
ramp of length l;
potential
energy = E_2

height h

angle A

object at height 0;
potential energy = E_1

$f = (E_2 - E_1)/l = g*m*h/l = g*m*\sin A$, where A is the angle of incline of the ramp (sin A = h/l)

Example 2: A Roller Coaster

In designing a roller coaster, the first approximation can ignore air drag and friction on the track, because (with the exception of the final braking) they are both small in comparison to the weight of the roller coaster with its passengers.

At the top height h_1, when the ride starts, its potential energy E_1 is:

$E_1 = g * m * h_1$

When, during a ride, a roller coaster drops to a height $h < h_1$, its potential energy decreases to:

$$E = g * m * h$$

The difference is converted into its kinetic energy $E_k = m * v^2 / 2$. Here, v is the speed of the roller coaster measured in m / s.

Thus,

$$E_k = E_1 - E$$

so,

$$m * v^2/2 = g * m * h_1 - g * m * h$$

and finally,

$$v = \sqrt{[2 * g * (h_1 - h)]}$$

Notice that this formula doesn't depend on the mass m. This means that a fully loaded roller coaster doesn't go faster than one that is only half full.

Task

Find out about the heights h_1 of different roller coasters in the world and estimate their speeds at different heights.

Unit 3

Potential Energy

An object that falls from a height h hits the ground after time t, where
$$t = \sqrt{(2 * h / g)}$$
and g = 9.81 m/s/s, with a speed v,
$$v = g * t$$

So its kinetic energy is:
$$E_k = m * v^2 / 2$$
where m is its mass

Therefore,
$$E_k = m * (g * t)^2 / 2 = m * g^2 * t^2 / 2 = m * g^2 * [\sqrt{(2 * h / g)}]^2 / 2$$
$$= m * g^2 * (2 * h / g) / 2 = m * g * h$$

But m * g = w is the weight of the object, namely, the downward force due to gravity; and h is the distance covered when one lifts the object from ground level to a height h. The product of distance times force is work, and thus
$$\text{work} = w * h = m * g * h = E_k$$

So we have reached the conclusion that the kinetic energy of an object falling from a height h is equal to the work needed to lift the object to this height. The energy due to the location of the object above the ground is one form of energy, and it is called potential energy, namely, "stored" energy. Another example of potential energy is energy stored in a coiled spring that is sometimes used to power toy cars. Coiled springs were also used in the past to power watches. (Study some spring-powered toy cars and old alarm clocks and find information about old watches on the Internet.)

Here is the front of an old-fashioned alarm clock that has a coiled spring for its alarm.

Here is the back of the clock. You can see the spring on the upper right.

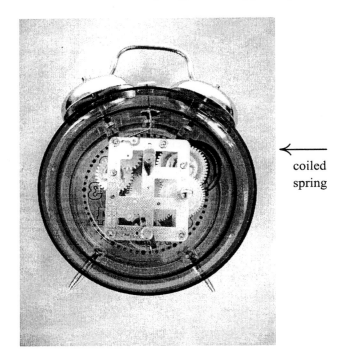

← coiled
spring

You can see the coiled spring in the toy car below.

Hydroelectric power plants tap the potential energy of water that is stored behind dams. The falling water changes its potential energy into kinetic energy that powers turbines, which turn engines, changing kinetic energy into electric energy.

Unit 4

Water Rockets

This unit should start outdoors. You need a simple water rocket for each three to five students, so each student can launch a rocket several times. We used the H_2O Rocket Set made by Lanard, which costs about $3 per set. (You can find inexpensive water rockets for sale on the Internet.)

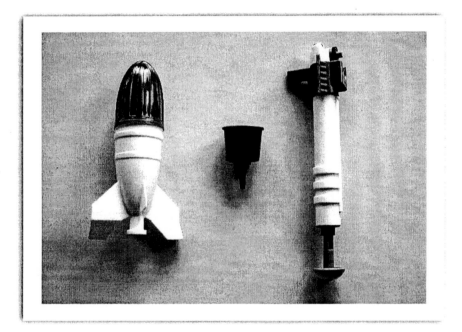

Each set contains one rocket, an air pump that also acts as a launcher, and a funnel for filling the rocket with water. Instructions on the back are clear and easy to follow. The amount of water that is used is very small, so the rockets are safe and not messy. Rockets should be given IDs so they don't get mixed up during the experiment. Students also need a stopwatch and measuring tape.

As a preliminary task, students may simply learn to launch their rockets. After they get really familiar with the toy, ask them to write:

1. A concise but detailed description of the rocket and the launching procedure.
2. The physical principles that explain what happens.

This second assignment should be preceded by a discussion of the relevant physics and possibly an additional reading assignment about "how rockets work."

Relevant Concepts and Units of Measurement

force	1 newton = 1 kgm/s^2 (kilogram meter per second squared);
weight	a force exerted on an object by the earth's gravity;
acceleration	m/s^2 (meters per second squared);
velocity	m/s (meters per second);
momentum	m * v (mass times velocity) measured in kgm/s;
energy	kgm^2/s^2 (kilogram meters per second squared)

Force, acceleration, velocity, and momentum are vectors. They have a direction. Energy is a scalar—one number can completely describe it.

Energy can take many forms:
- kinetic energy = (mass * speed^2) / 2
- potential energy of an object above the ground relative to ground level = weight * (height above the ground)
- work = force * (length of its path)
- internal energy of a gas under high pressure (a form of potential energy relative to atmospheric pressure)
- heat

The Energy Balance for the Launch of a Rocket

1. Pumping air is doing work.
2. This work increases the pressure of the air in the rocket and, therefore, transforms into the internal energy of that air.
3. When the rocket is launched, the air inside expands, getting back to atmospheric pressure. Its internal energy converts into the kinetic energy of the rocket and the kinetic energy of the jettisoned water.
4. During the flight up, the rocket is slowing down, changing its kinetic energy into potential energy relative to ground level.
5. During the fall, the rocket's potential energy converts back into kinetic energy.
6. Finally, when the rocket hits the ground, its kinetic energy is dissipated in different ways and at least part of it is transformed into heat.

Force

The speed of the rocket on the launcher is zero. The force of the expanding air at the launch pushes the rocket up and pushes the water down. This force accelerates the rocket to its flying speed.

Momentum

The principle of preservation of momentum tells us that the momentum of the rocket directed up would be the same as the momentum of the water directed down. Because the speed of the water stream is quite limited, if its mass is too small, its total momentum is also small. In such a case the momentum of the rocket will also be minimal. In the case of no water, the only thing that is pushed down is a little air, and the rocket will barely move.

An Experiment with Data Collection

Each group launches its rocket several times. They should try to shoot straight up, but a reasonable variety is expected.

For each launch, they record:
- the height at which the rocket was held at launch time, with an accuracy of 10 cm.
- the distance from the launching point to the place where the rocket first hits the ground, with an accuracy (depending on distance) of 0.5 to 1.5 meters.
- the time from the launch to the moment the rocket first hits the ground.

Before (or after) the experiment, students should also weigh the empty rocket (in grams).

Questions That Can Be Answered without Much Theory

1. Is there a relationship among the variables measured? If so, what is it?

   The answer is no. The difference between launches from different heights will not be big enough to stand out. Also the horizontal distance would be more dependent on the angle of launch and the wind than on the time of flight. In general, the time of flight will decrease if the rocket is shot more horizontally, but this will not show up in the data for launches that are close to vertical.

The Theoretical Questions to Be Discussed

1. The momentum of the flying rocket as it starts is equal to the momentum of the expelled water, but the rocket has a direction that is opposite to the water (the sum of the two momentums is zero). Both the momentum of the rocket and the momentum of the water are the result of the force of the expanding air. Because of the force of gravity, the momentum decreases as the rocket moves up. At the top of the trajectory the momentum is zero, and it increases again when the rocket falls down. What is the momentum of the rocket after the launch (and at the time it hits the ground)? Can it be (approximately) computed from the data?
2. The rocket moves under the force of gravity, air drag, and the force of the wind after it empties. What is its predicted trajectory, without the wind and without drag, and what is the influence of these additional forces?
3. What is the source of energy for the water rocket, and what happens to it?

In the next units we use the data we collected (launch height, distance from launch site to landing site, and time of flight) to predict how high our rocket flew.

Unit 5

How High Does a Rocket Fly?

The Practical Value of Formulas That Are Used in Physics

Question

When you launch a water rocket, how high does it fly?

Let's consider some methods for measuring the altitude that is reached by a rocket.

1. Launch the rocket next to a tall building of known height (measure its height if necessary). The floors correspond to a marking on a vertical ruler. Have observers who are standing rather far from the building to tell which floor the rocket reached.

   Disadvantages
   - It is difficult to find the right locality.
   - If the building is not high enough or has a balcony, you may lose your rocket.

2. Put the observers in pairs at known distances, d, from the launch site. One of them will use an aiming device, which consists of a straight stick or a ruler tied to a protractor (or a straw taped to one), and a plumb line hanging down from the hole in the protractor.

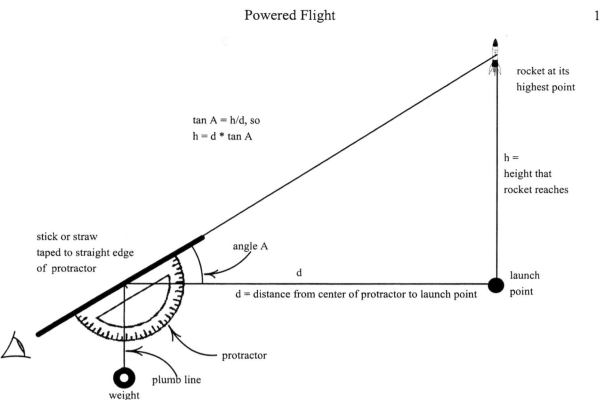

One of the observers tries to point the stick toward the highest point of the rocket's trajectory, and the other observer reads the angle A between the stick and the plumb line. The height

$$h = d/(\tan A).$$

Disadvantages
- You need a large open space because observers must stand far from the launch site.
- Aiming the stick is neither precise nor easy.

3. Use a stopwatch to measure the time t of the flight.
   The time during which the water is ejected from the rocket is very short, so most of the time the only forces acting on the rocket are gravity and air drag. If the air drag is small, it can be ignored. The rocket is making its whole flight in time t, and it falls down from its greatest height in time:

$$t' = t / 2$$

The time t' of free fall and the height h are related by the equation:

$$h = 9.81 * t'^2 / 2$$

Time is measured in seconds, height in meters, and 9.81 is the acceleration due to the earth's gravitational attraction, measured in m/s/s.

So you can measure the total time t that the rocket is in flight, divide this t by two to get the time of free fall t', and then plug t' into the equation:

$$h = 9.81 * t'^2 / 2$$

This can be approximated by $h \approx 5 * t'^2$.
(It is important that the rocket be launched in a *vertical* position, not at an angle!)

Disadvantage
- Water rockets are rather light and bulky. So in spite of their aerodynamic shape, air drag can be a significant factor. This would result in overestimating the actual height. The heavier and sleeker fuel-powered rockets are less influenced by air drag. But they fly faster (and higher), and the drag is stronger at higher speeds.

Remark

1. In this unit we show the use of formulas, and not how they were found.

Unit 6

More about Rockets

The formula students will use to estimate the height of the flight is:

$$h = g / 2 * (t / 2)^2$$

Here, h is the height reached, and t is the total time of the flight.

This formula uses the fact that the time the rocket takes to go up and the time it takes to fall to the ground are the same, which is true with the following assumptions:

1. The only force that acts on the rocket during its flight is gravity.
2. The starting point is just at the ground.

These assumptions are not true; they are only approximate. Namely, the other forces are not large enough to make much difference, and also the height at which the rocket is launched is not very influential.

But the deviation from these assumptions creates systematic errors, which we'll briefly look at now.

1. The role of air drag.
   Air drag slows the rocket down, so it doesn't travel quite as far as predicted in time t; so h is overestimated. We have no way of predicting the size of this effect theoretically. We only hope it is small.
2. At the beginning of the flight, the thrust of the ejected water accelerates the rocket from a speed of zero to its flight speed, so the initial speed upward, v_0, is reached at some distance above the launching point.

   My estimate from the water spray indicates that the initial speed is reached approximately 0.5 m about the launcher (but this estimate may be quite off the mark). It also shows that water is ejected almost instantly.

   When we launch the rocket while we are standing up, the launcher is held approximately 1 m above the floor. Thus, the total effect is as if the rocket were launched from a height $h_0 = 1.5$ m, and as if the total time were shorter by a small but unknown amount t_0 (the time of the water spray). The height h_0 can be made smaller by kneeling or lying down during the launch.

   We are not going to deal with these deviations in our computations because the systematic errors that are due to air drag and to the height h_0 of the launching site have a tendency to cancel each other out.

We ignore t_0, and compute the effect due to h_0.

We know h_0 and t, and we want to know h.
A one-way trip from h_0 to h takes time:

$$t_1 = \sqrt{[2 * (h - h_0) / g]}$$

A one-way trip from h to 0 (ground level) takes time:

$$t_2 = \sqrt{(2 * h / g)}$$

Thus, a round trip from h_0 to 0 takes:

(a) $t = t_1 + t_2 = \sqrt{[2 * (h - h_0) / g]} + \sqrt{(2 * h / g)}$

We know t, h_0, and g, so we can find h using SOLVER on the TI-83 Plus calculator. Here is how to do it:

Define these variables:

Use Y for the unknown height h that the rocket reaches

H for h_0, the launching height

G for g, the force due to gravity (9.81 m/s/s)

T for t, the time of the rocket's flight

In the SOLVER, enter

Eqn: $0 = \sqrt{[2 * (Y - H) / G]} + \sqrt{(2 * Y / G)} - T$

Here is how it looks on the calculator screen:

```
EQUATION SOLVER
eqn:0=√(2*(Y-H)/
G)+√(2*Y/G)-T
```

Initialize H, G, and T, and solve for Y. If you enter H in meters, T in seconds, and G = 9.81, you will get the unknown height Y in meters. Here is a screen dump when H = 1.25 meters, G = 9.81 m/s/s, and T = 3 seconds. Y, the predicted height of the rocket, is 11 2/3 meters.

```
√(2*(Y-H)/G)+…=0
 Y=11.670098680…
 H=1.25
 G=9.81
 T=3
 bound={-1E99,1…
```

We can also estimate h from this equation, which we get from (a) above:

$$g * t^2 = [\sqrt{(2 * (h - h_0))} + \sqrt{(2 * h)}]^2$$
$$= 2 * (h - h_0) + 2 * \sqrt{[4 * (h - h_0) * h]} + 2 * h$$

Factoring out 2 * h, we have

$$g * t^2 = 2 * h * [1 - h_0 / h + 2 * \sqrt{(1 - h_0 / h)} + 1]$$

We substitute $1 - 0.5 * (h_0 / h)$ for $\sqrt{(1 - h_0 / h)}$, since $1 - 0.5 * (h_0 / h) \approx \sqrt{(1 - h_0 / h)}$, and we have:

$$g * t^2 \approx 2 * h * (4 - 2 * h_0/h)$$
$$g * t^2 \approx 8 * h - 4 * h_0$$

Thus,

$$g / 2 * (t / 2)^2 = (g * t^2) / 8 \approx (8 * h - 4 * h_0)/8 = h - h_0 / 2$$

Therefore, the expression $g / 2 (t / 2)^2$ underestimates the actual h by $h_0 / 2$.

Note that when we compute $h = g / 2 \, (t / 2)^2$ for the values we used with the TI-83 calculator above, namely $g = 9.81$ m/s/s and $t = 3$, we get $h = 11.03635$. Adding one-half of the launch height h_0, or one-half of 1.25 meters = 0.625 meters, we have $h = 11.66$ meters as the predicted height the rocket reached.

Conclusion

The systematic errors that are due to air drag and to the height h0 of the launching site have a tendency to cancel each other out.

Chapter 9

Magnetism and Electricity

Unit 1

Physical units

One discouraging feature of physics is the number of units you have to deal with. You have volts, watts, amperes, pascals, newtons, joules, dynes, ergs, and many more. Even to memorize their names is a big task, and learning their definitions and conversion tables is almost impossible. Fortunately, this encyclopedic type of knowledge is not essential, even for specialists. But it is convenient to have access to a hard copy of an encyclopedia of science for quick reference, or to have access to the Internet for quick searches. For example, http://www.unc.edu/~rowlett/units/ gives you easy access to all units and their descriptions, and a Google search for "units of measurement" reveals many more. Another site is http://www.ex.ac.uk/cimt/dictunit/dictunit.htm.

In order to measure quantities, we compare their amounts to some "standard" amounts called units. The system of units used in science is quite uniform because all scientists have adopted the metric system.

In statics and dynamics we need only three "basic" units:

1 meter (m)	for measuring length
1 second (s)	for measuring time
1 kilogram (kg)	for measuring mass, which is a property of matter

Other units, which measure other quantities, are defined in terms of these three. For example:

1 m/s	measures speed
1 m/s/s	measures acceleration
1 newton = kg * m/s/s	measures force
1 joule = m * newton	measures work and energy
1 pascal = newton / (m^2)	measures pressure
1 watt = 1 joule/s	measures power

But these three basic units—kg, m, and s—are not sufficient for measuring electric and magnetic phenomena. Electric charge is a different property of matter, independent of its mass, its position in space, or its movement in time. So we need a new basic unit that measures these phenomena. There are two main candidates:

1 coulomb (C)	measures the amount of electric charge
1 ampere (A)	measures the flow of electric charge

Electric charge seems to be more "basic," but its flow is easier to measure. In either case, it is easy to get one from the other:

1 C = A * s
1 A = 1 C / s

Thus, 1 ampere is a flow of 1 coulomb of electric charge per second.

Thus, most measurements that deal with electricity and magnetism use units that are constructed not only from kilograms, meters, and seconds, but also from amperes (or coulombs). Usually we do not have any good intuition about the meanings of these measurements, and we build an intuition only slowly by getting familiar with their use.

An Example

1 volt (V)   = 1 watt/ampere
                  = 1 (joule/s)/ampere
                  = 1 (newton * m)/s/ampere
                  = 1 (kg * m/s/s) * m/s/ampere
                  = 1 (kg * m2)/(ampere * s3)

We measure electric potential in volts. The electric current that is delivered to your home has a potential of 110 volts. Small AAA batteries are 1.5-volt batteries. The more powerful batteries that you can buy in a supermarket have 9 volts. How many volts does a car battery have?

But what does electric potential mean?

        1 watt is a measure of power.
Power is measured by the amount of work done per unit of time. Thus,
        1 watt = 1 joule/s
is the ability to do 1 joule of work per second.

One watt is not very much. If you lift 4 kg (a little more than 1 gallon) of milk from the floor and put it on a shelf at the level of your face in one second (which is not a very big feat), you have displayed a power of approximately 60 watts.

Sixty watts is also the power that is displayed by a 60-watt light bulb to produce light (and heat).

The power of electric current depends not only on its amount (measured in amperes), but also on another property which we call potential.

        power = (amount of current) * (electric potential)

The units are related as follows:
        1 watt = 1 ampere * volt

An analogy, which should not be taken literally, is:
The power of a waterfall depends on the amount of water that is flowing in a given time interval together with the height of the waterfall.

When we measure electric potential, we really measure its difference between two levels. So in a 1.5-volt battery, the difference between the + end and the – end of the battery is 1.5 volts.

Warning

Power is also a measure of the amount of damage that can be done in a unit of time. So, small batteries are safe; electric current delivered to houses is moderately dangerous; and high power lines are extremely dangerous.

Dimensional Analysis

Analyzing relationships among units of measurements was, and often is, called "dimensional analysis." Knowing the relationships among units not only is essential for understanding relations among quantities, but also provides many insights into otherwise "mysterious" phenomena.

The mathematical theory handling units is just algebra. Units are just treated as any other algebraic variables or constants. Physical units are actually some chosen constant quantities to which other quantities are compared.

Most of the common physical units can be constructed from units for mass, length, and time. Here we will use the units of kilogram (kg), meter (m), and second (s). Any other set would do, but this one is the most common in science.

Let's look more carefully at pressure. From above, we know 1 pascal = 1 newton/(m2) measures pressure. So pressure is force divided by area. But we can rewrite it:
$$(kgm/s^2)/m^2 = (kgm/s)/m^2/s$$
This means that pressure can be viewed as momentum per unit area per unit of time. What does this mean?

The modern theory of gases shows that a gas consists of particles of matter freely flying and bouncing off of each other and off of the objects they come in contact with.

Each moving particle has its momentum, which depends on its mass and its speed. Particles bounce off of objects like ping pong balls. Bouncing changes their momentum by changing their direction.

Thus, the pressure the gas puts on the surface of an object is the amount of change of momentum of the gas particles that hit a unit of area in a unit of time.

What Is the Conclusion?

By analyzing physical units, we can get some insight about the relationships among physical quantities.

Unit 2

Introduction to Magnetic Forces

Materials

On each table there should be a set of magnets, including one "slab" magnet, several "rings," a "horseshoe," and possibly some "spheres," together with a selection of nails, including large ones, and other iron objects such as nuts, and at least one directional compass. (Compasses with transparent plastic bottoms are the best for this purpose.)

Each magnet has two ends, called poles, north and south. If you put two opposite poles of two magnets near each other, they attract each other; but two poles that are the same (either both south or both north) repel each other.

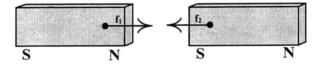

Two opposite poles of two magnets attract each other.

Two poles that are the same (either both south or both north) repel each other.

The end of the needle of a compass that points north (the needle is a magnet!) is called its north pole. Thus if you put the compass near a magnet, the north end of the needle will point to the south pole of the magnet (opposites attract!).

Task

1. Find the north and south poles of your magnets. Observe that the poles of the horseshoe magnet are at the ends of a bent slab of iron.

2. Put ring magnets on a pencil (or on a ring stand) and see what happens depending on their orientation.

Magnets attract and repel only those objects that contain a considerable amount of iron, nickel, or cobalt. An object attracted by a magnet also becomes a magnet, at least temporarily.

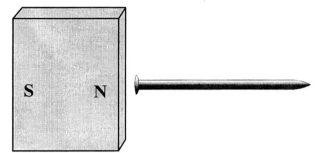

3. Check with a compass that the sharp point of the nail is now its north pole. See that it attracts small iron objects.
4. Take a few iron nuts of different sizes, weigh them, and use a spring scale to pull them from a slab magnet. In this way you can measure (in newtons) the strength of the magnetic force that holds a nut to a slab magnet and its relation to the mass of the nut (in kilograms). Record your findings.

An Example of Data

(Data for blue magnet with handle) Hexagonal nut number	Weight of nut in grams	Force in newtons required to pull nut away from magnet (averaged over five trials)
1	50.0	200 g ≈ 2.0 newtons
2	32.0	180 g ≈ 1.8 newtons
3	14.5	140 g ≈ 1.4 newtons
4	4.5	100 g ≈ 1.0 newton
5	3.0	80 g ≈ 0.8 newton

Graphing the data using Excel, we have:

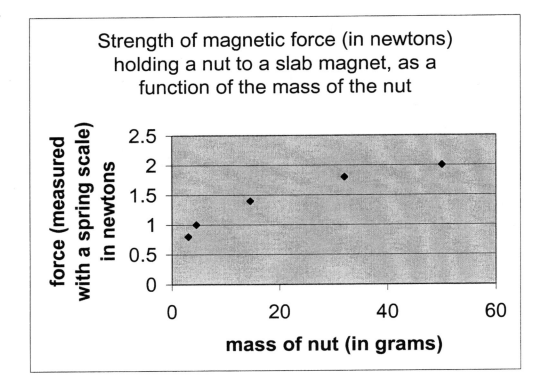

Unit 3

The Structure of a Magnet

Experiment

Materials

- several slab or ring magnets
- a nut or other iron object
- and spring scale

If you put slab or ring magnets together, with opposite poles touching, you create one bigger magnet. Is this composite magnet stronger than a one-slab (one-ring) magnet?

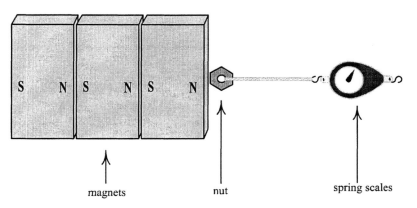

magnets   nut   spring scales

Task

Record the data (use newtons as units of force).

Many small magnets that are aligned together can form bigger stronger magnets. This is the principle underlying the magnetic property of iron. Each atom of iron is a small magnet with a south and north pole. Usually these "mini-magnets" are arranged randomly, pointing in all directions, and the magnetic force fields that are generated by them cancel each other out.

But some natural iron ores and many artificial alloys have a "crystal-like" structure in which all atoms are aligned, with their north poles pointing in one direction and their south poles pointing in the opposite direction. These pieces are magnets.

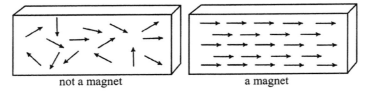

In a normal piece of iron, atoms can easily change their directions. Thus, if you put a piece of iron next to a magnet, its atoms align in the direction of the magnetic forces, just as the needle of a compass did in one of our previous experiments. So, the piece of iron becomes a magnet too. But when you move the magnet away from the iron, the atoms in the iron rearrange themselves after a while into a random pattern, and the piece of iron again stops being a magnet.

Heating a piece of iron speeds up this process. Thus, if you take a magnet and heat it on a gas or electric burner, it will lose its magnetic property because heat will move the atoms from their orderly positions. (Do this to your magnet only if you do not mind losing it as a magnet. Be careful! Hot iron makes nasty burns.)

Unit 4

Magnetic Fields

A "slab" or "bar" magnet is a brick-shaped magnet, usually with a long plastic handle.

For this lesson, each table should have at least two slab magnets, at least two magnetic (directional) compasses, and a protractor for measuring angles. We also used wooden skewers to help us lay out the angles. A paper bag is needed for the "magic trick."

Experiment 1

In this experiment the magnet will stand on the table upright (with its handle up). Place the compass close to it, as shown in picture 1.

Picture 1

Now rotate the magnet around its vertical axis by angle A. What happens to the magnetic needle? Does it rotate? By what angle? You may keep a chart of where the compass points as a function of the angle of the magnet. Here are some data we collected, together with photos of our experiment.

Picture 2

Picture 3

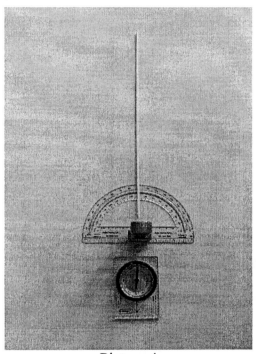

Picture 4

Picture number	Angle of magnet	Angle of compass
1	0°	0°
2	–45°	20°
3	–90°	90°
4	–180°	180°

In picture 4, the direction of the compass is NS, but this time the south end of the compass needle points toward the magnet, whereas in picture 1, the north end of the needle pointed toward the magnet.

What is the role of the distance between the magnet and the compass? Move the compass closer to or farther from the magnet, and collect data again as above.

Does the direction of the magnet relative to the earth's magnetic north matter? If the compass is close to the magnet, no. But if the compass is a meter or more from the magnet, then the compass is not affected by the little magnet, but only by the earth's magnet.

A "Magic Trick"

Put a compass on a table and move the magnet around inside a paper bag, so it is invisible to children. The needle will still rotate. Ask, "What do I have in the bag?"

Experiment 2

You need two or more magnets and two or more compasses. Arrange them on a table in an "interesting" configuration. Then, as above, start rotating the magnets, choosing different angles for different magnets. Observe what happens to the magnetic needles on the compasses. It can be very complex. Can you turn the magnets so that the two needles point in the same direction? In opposite directions? So that the two needles are perpendicular to each other?

About Magnetic Fields

Forces come in pairs. They are interactions between objects. Both the force of gravity and magnetic forces act over a distance. Thus, many objects that are interacting with one object can be located at different distances and can be quite inaccessible.

In order to study such effects, we introduce the concept of a *force field*. It is the combined effect of all the forces that would act on an object that is located at a given position in space. To measure the strength and direction of the field, we put an object that acts as a probe at several locations in space, and at each location we measure the direction and strength of the forces acting on it.

The force field of gravity near the surface of the earth is not interesting. It points downward and has a strength, as measured by its pull on one gram of mass, of 0.00981 newtons.

But the force field of gravity is of utmost importance for spacecraft that are exploring our solar system. One has to take into consideration the force field that is a combination of the pull of the sun, the earth, the moon, and the other planets. This force field is changing all the time because of planetary motion.

The study of magnetic forces is never simple. Even the simplest magnet has two poles, and the magnetic needle of a compass also has two poles. So the simplest interaction involves four forces—two of them are repelling (between the two north poles and the two south poles), and two of them are attracting (between the south and north poles of the magnet and the needle). In our experiments we will use a (magnetic) compass to measure the direction of the magnetic field. We will not measure its strength.

Experiment 3

Prepare a one square inch dot grid on a piece of paper that is at least one square foot in size. Attach it to a table with tape so it doesn't move during the experiment. (We taped together several sheets to cover a much larger area.) Mark the direction toward north with an arrow. Stand a slab magnet upright in one corner (and mark its position on the paper, indicating its south and north poles). Put the center of your compass on each dot, observe the direction of the magnetic needle, and draw an arrow through the dot in the direction of the north pole of the needle. (You may place a protractor under the compass, to help you get an accurate straight line after you remove the compass.)

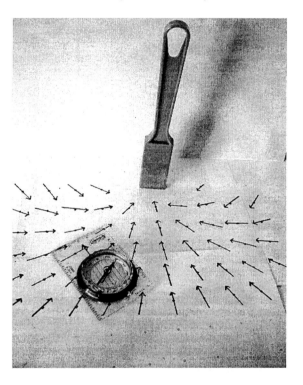

The pattern of arrows shows the directions of the magnetic force field generated by the magnet and the earth. (More precisely, we draw only the horizontal component of the forces. The actual directions would not be just horizontal, but slightly slanted. But we cannot measure such a slant with a standard compass needle.)

Unit 5

Magnetic Sand and Patterns with Iron Filings

Activities for the Early Grades

Experiment 1: Collecting Iron Dust

Materials

- Strong bar or horseshoe magnets
- handheld microscopes or strong magnifying glasses
- dry desert sand. (Instead of bringing sand inside, children can do the first part outside the school building.)

Gathering Dust

When you move a magnet through sand, you see that a dark-colored dust and small grains of dark sand adhere to it. Shake the excess sand gently and bring the magnets with the dust that is adhering inside.

Observing

Look at the dust through a hand-held microscope or a strong magnifying glass. You observe that the grains of dust stick not only to the magnet but also to each other (the dust forms "streaks"). Their behavior is similar to iron filings, but they are smaller.

Explaining

What you observe is small particles of sand that contain enough iron ore (iron oxides) to be attracted to a magnet.

Remarks

1. Instead of throwing out the magnetic dust, scrape it off of the magnets with two small index cards and save it in a small jar for a future use.
2. Focusing a handhold microscope is tricky. Be sure that all children master this skill.

Experiment 2: Patterns with Iron Filings

Take a stick magnet or a u-shaped (horseshoe) magnet, but not a slab magnet. Put it on a table. Put an index card on top of the magnet. The card must be horizontal. Sprinkle iron filings on the card. (You may use the iron ore from experiment 1.) Tap the card lightly with your finger. You should see the lines of a force field.

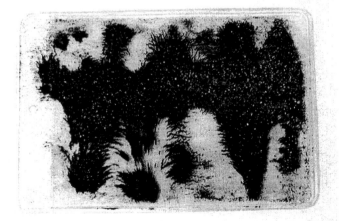

We found stiff clear plastic "pockets" or envelopes at a craft store, put iron filings in them, and sealed them with tape. With these pockets you can play with the iron filings without making a mess since the filings will stay contained in the pockets. Here is an example:

Unit 6

Simulation of Lines of a Magnetic Field

This simulation, made on a TI-83 Plus graphing calculator, shows the lines along which a compass needle would align when it is put close to two magnetic poles. You choose the position of the poles, which may be either on the screen or outside of it, and you also decide if the poles are the same (NN or SS) or opposite (NS). The resolution is rather crude, so the picture is not very clear. (See http://www.colorado.edu/physics/2000/applets/forcefield.html for an interactive simulation of a force field.)

When you run the program, you are first prompted for the position of the poles (you enter them as Lists, and the values do not have to be integers), and then you are prompted for the "signs of the poles" (to which you answer, 1 = "same" or –1 = "opposite").

Examples

POLES
?{16,0}   This pole is off the screen (the visible values are between
?{0,0}   –15 and 15 on the x-axis, and between –10 and 10 on the y-axis).
SIGNS
?-1   The poles are opposite (N S).

Here is the picture:

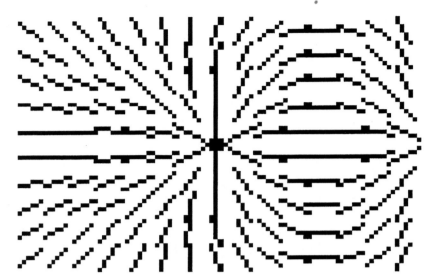

POLES
?{-5.1,-3.5}
?{7.8,2.6}
SIGNS
?1   The poles are the same (NN or SS).

Here is the picture:

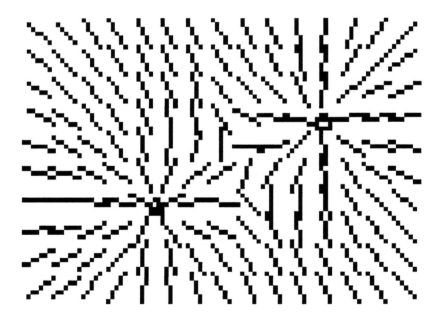

Program	Comments

PROGRAM:MAGFIELD
:ZStandard
:ZSquare
:ClrDraw
:AxesOff
:Disp "POLES?"
:Input L1   The location of the poles is stored in L1 and L2.
:Input L2
:Disp"SIGNS?"
:Input S   S = -1 means "opposite", S = 1 means "same."
:Circle(L1(1),L1(2),.5)   The poles are drawn.
:Circle(L2(1),L2(2),.5)
:For(X,-14,14,2)   Lines will be drawn through the points (X,Y).
:For(Y,-9,9,2)
:(X-L1(1))2+(Y-L1(1))2→D   Squares of the distances (X,Y)
:(X-L2(1))2+(Y-L2(1))2→E   to the poles are stored in D and E.
:If D>.8 and E>.8   Lines are not drawn through the poles.
:Then
:({X,Y}-L1)/D^(3/2)+   The sum of the forces at (X,Y) is computed
S({X,Y}-L2)/E^(3/2)→L3   and stored in L3.

:L3(1)2+L3(2)2→F   The square of the magnitude of the forces is in F.
:1.2L3/(√(F)+.001) →L3   The direction of the line at (X,Y) is in L2.
:Line(X-L3(1),Y-L3(2),   The line is drawn.
X+L3(1),Y+L3(2))

:END   End of "If."
:END   End of "For Y."
:END   End of "For X."

(Each new program instruction begins with a colon (:). Notice that two of the program instructions above span not one line on the screen, but two.)

Unit 7

A Chaotic Pendulum

Introduction

Some people think that science deals mainly with regular and predictable patterns of events. But regular and predictable patterns are really the exception, and chaotic, unpredictable patterns are encountered much more often. Doing a simple experiment can give us some insight as to why this is so.

Experiment

Put a few, or several, ring or slab magnets on the floor, some of them with their south poles up and others with their north poles up. Make a pendulum with a weight made from a small horseshoe magnet or a ring magnet or a ball magnet, and thin, soft, strong string. (You may need to use tape to fasten the magnet to the string.) Hang the pendulum from a chopstick that has been fastened to the edge of a table above the magnets. (The hanging magnet should be approximately half an inch above the magnets on the floor). Swing the pendulum and see what happens. Play with different configurations.

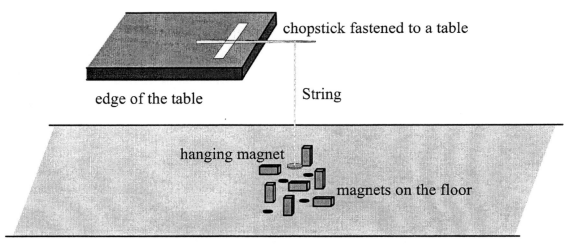

chopstick fastened to a table

edge of the table   String

hanging magnet

magnets on the floor

floor

Explanation

The magnets on the floor cannot move because they are pressed down by gravity, and the friction between them and the floor prevents them from sliding. But the hanging magnet can move. So let's list the forces that change its momentum and, in this way, control its velocity.

1. Force of gravity.
2. Pull of the string.
3. Four forces acting on the hanging magnet as the result of an interaction with each magnet on the floor:
    a) the pull of the south pole on the north pole
    b) the pull of the north pole on the south pole
    c) the repulsive force between the north poles
    d) the repulsive force between the south poles

Thus, with, let's say, five magnets on the floor, there are twenty-two forces on the hanging magnet acting in different directions and with different strengths; both their directions and strengths vary, depending on the exact location of the swinging magnet. Some of these forces partially cancel each other out, and some reinforce each other.

Such a pattern of forces can lead to extremely complex, chaotic, and unpredictable movement of the swinging magnet.

General Conclusion

If only a few forces influence the movement of an object, the object moves along a predictable and quite regular trajectory. When the number of forces increases and if the forces do not cancel each other out, then the movement of the object becomes complex, erratic, and unpredictable.

Unit 8

Making a Closed Circuit

Experiment

Materials

Students work in groups of two or three. Each group has:
- one AA (1.5-volt) battery
- two pieces of insulated wire
- a small light bulb

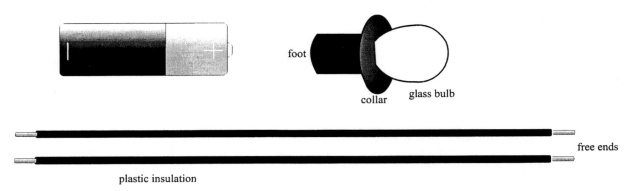

Task: Light the Bulb

Solution

Put a bulb and battery on the table. Touch one end of the battery and the foot of the bulb with the ends of one wire and touch the other end of the battery and the collar of the bulb with the end of the other wire.

You have created a closed circuit,
       battery–wire–bulb–wire–battery,
and this enables the flow of electric current.
(You may also create a closed circuit with battery–bulb–wire–battery.)

Remark

1. Many children believe that the current flows from the battery to the bulb in a flashlight. They are surprised that just touching the foot of the bulb to the plus end of the battery is not sufficient to light the bulb.

Unit 9

Electromagnetic Forces

Interactions between Electric Currents and Magnets

Experiment

Materials

Students work in small groups. Each group has:
- one 1.5 volt battery
- a long piece of wire
- a magnetic compass

The Setting

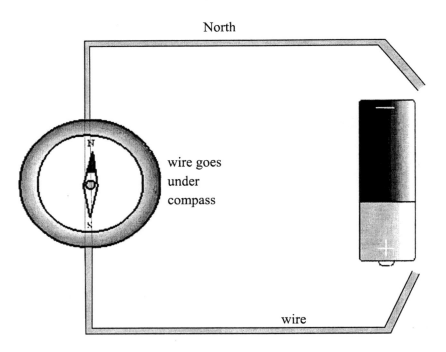

(The wire is bent into the shape of a square, with one side partly open; the battery is in the opening, with the ends of the wire close by.)

1. Start with the left side of the wire going under the compass. Touch the ends of the battery with the ends of the wire, closing the circuit. Observe that the needle turns approximately 90°.

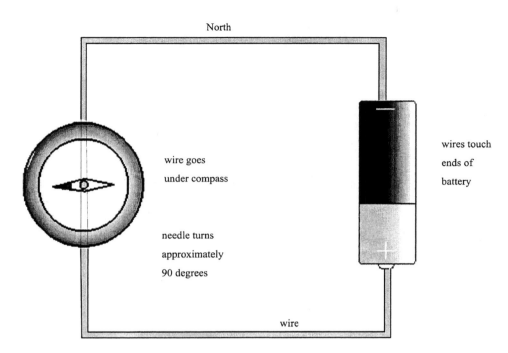

Note the direction of the north end of the needle.

2. Change the direction of the battery and repeat the experiment. Note the direction of the north end of the needle.

3. Now put the wire over the top of the compass and repeat the experiment twice, putting the battery in both directions.

How do you interpret these four results?

Explanation

Electric current creates a magnetic force field around the wire. (The wire is shown as a dot in the diagram below. It is coming out of the page.)

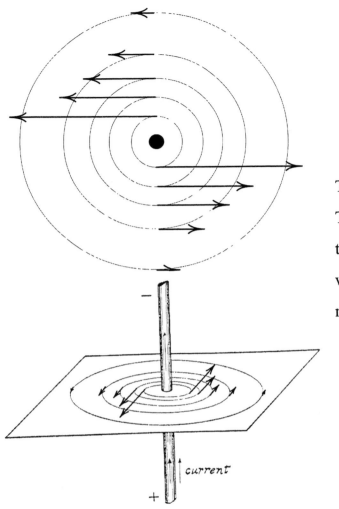

The arrows are vectors.
Their length represents
the strength of the field,
which we are not
measuring.

The direction (clockwise or counterclockwise) depends on the direction of the electric current. This force makes the magnetic needle (which is a magnet) turn in a direction that is perpendicular to the wire.

The forces acting between an electric current and a magnet are called electromagnetic forces. (Remember that if the electric current exerts a force on a magnet, then the magnet exerts a force of the same magnitude and in the opposite direction on the electric current.)

Now suppose we put two wires (that are connected to batteries) parallel to each other, with currents in opposite directions. The arrows indicating a force field add (as vectors), still forming loops around both wires and forming a strong field between them and a weak field outside. (The lines are dense between the wires, and they spread apart outside.)

The diagram shows a magnetic field. The two black dots represent two separate wires or two cross sections of the same wire. It is important that the direction of current is opposite in the two.

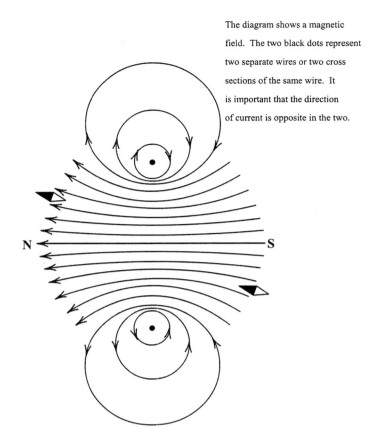

You see the same pattern if you look at a longitudinal cross section of a coiled wire. Notice that the direction of the force field is the same in the picture above and the one below.

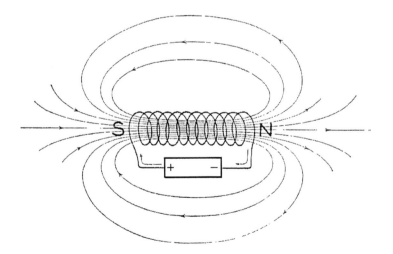

You have a strong field inside the coil, pointing in one direction. It loops to the outside, creating a weak spread-out field in the opposite direction. (The lines are very close together inside, and they are spread apart outside.)

Now if we put an iron core such as a nail inside the coiled wire, the field inside the loop is strong enough to align the atoms, turning the piece of iron into a magnet.

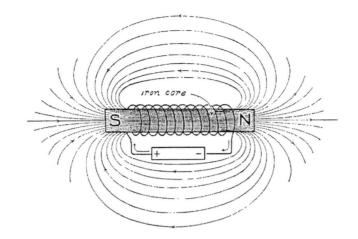

Unit 10

Electromagnets

We already know that an electric current flowing through a wire creates a field of magnetic forces around the wire. This field turns a magnetic needle in a direction that is determined by the direction of the current and the position of the needle relative to the wire.

We also know that the difference between a magnet and just any piece of iron is that in a magnet, all (or most) iron atoms (which are themselves mini-magnets) are aligned in one direction, so their magnetic fields reinforce each other instead of canceling out.

We combine these two pieces of knowledge to make an electromagnet.

Materials

- 1.5-volt battery
- several inches of thin insulated copper wire
- a thin iron nail or a (large) paper clip (softer iron is better)
- pliers
- iron filings or a paper clip, together with a compass, are needed for testing.

Construction

Cut a piece of paper clip approximately one inch long and straighten it with pliers. Coil the wire very tightly around this piece of iron (or around a nail), leaving two ends that are long enough to reach both ends of the battery.

coiled wire

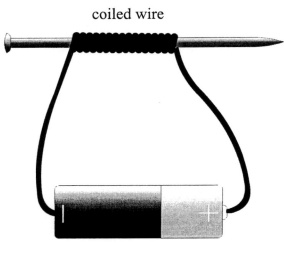

Testing

When you close the circuit and the current starts flowing, the core of the electromagnet (the nail or the piece of paper clip) becomes a magnet. (Test it to see if it will pick up some iron filings or a paper clip, or if it will affect the needle of a compass. See the photo below.) Testing is easier if you use a long piece of wire so that the battery can be kept several inches away! The reason for this is that batteries contain iron, so keeping them farther away when you test your electromagnet with a compass works better and this requires longer wires. Also, more coils make the electromagnet work better because they make the magnetic field that is generated by the current in the iron core stronger.

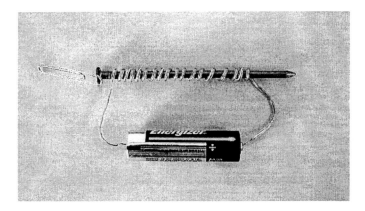

When you reverse the battery and change the direction of the current, the north and south poles of the electromagnet reverse. (Test this with a compass.)

When the current stops flowing, the core still preserves some of its magnetic property, but it starts losing it. (You may speed up this process by heating the core with a lighted match.)

Explanation

The magnetic field of a coiled wire is the strongest along the axis of the "cylinder" and weaker outside.

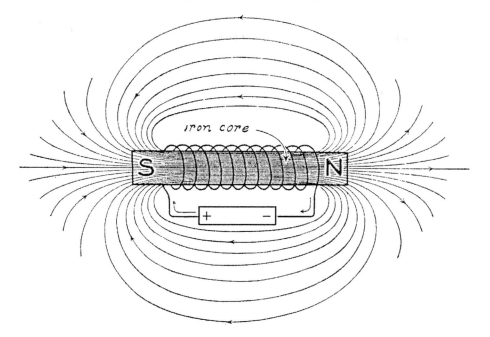

This field is not very strong, but it is strong enough to align atoms in the iron core, so the core becomes a magnet. When the current reverses, the atoms flip over and become aligned with their north poles, facing in the opposite direction. When the current stops flowing, the atoms slowly lose their alignment and become randomly oriented again (heat speeds up this process.)

Electromagnets have many applications. They can be made much stronger than any magnets that are found in nature. They are cheaper. And they can be switched on and off instantly.

Unit 11

General Information about Electricity

Basic Properties of Matter

Mass is a basic property of matter. Two objects interact by gravitational attraction, which is proportional to the product of their masses divided by the square of their distance from each other.

Electricity, or more exactly, electric charge, which we sometimes experience when we touch a doorknob, is another basic property of matter. But there are big differences between these two basic properties (mass and electric charge).

Electric Charges

Electric charges come in two kinds, which we (arbitrarily) label positive (+) and negative (-). Some elementary particles of matter have positive charges, some have negative charges, and some have no charge at all.

Two objects that have opposite charges interact by attracting each other. But two objects that have the same charge repel each other. The strength of these forces is proportional to the product of the charges and inversely proportional to the square of their distance. These forces are called "electrostatic."

Electrostatic forces are much stronger than the gravitational force. Gravitation is observed when we deal with objects as massive as planets or suns, so it is of special interest to astronomers. Electric charges are so strong that they are visible on the micro-level. They are responsible for many, but not all, chemical reactions, so they are of interest to chemists and physicists. Fortunately, because the effects of positive and negative charges cancel each other out, we live in an electrically neutral environment, and the strength of these forces is observed only when there is an excess of positive or negative charges. Such an excess is responsible for lightning and is also the cause of accidents, when someone touches a live wire.

Magnetic Fields

But that is not all. When electric charges move (moving charges form an electric current), they create a field of magnetic forces. We observed this in a previous unit by putting a compass next to a wire that was carrying electric current. These magnetic forces occur only when charges are moving.

A static charge creates no magnetic force. This connection between electricity and magnetism is the basis for most of the important applications of electricity.

Electric Power

Electric current can do work. It can generate heat, make light, and power machinery and appliances. This shows that electric current carries energy because energy is the ability to do work. Electric energy is a different kind of energy than the potential and kinetic energy that we have discussed so far. But it is a very mobile kind of energy. It is delivered to our houses constantly through quite thin copper wires. When we pay our electric bills, we pay for the energy that is used in our household. The unit used to measure electric energy delivered to homes is the kilowatt hour.

> 1 kWh = $3.6*10^6$ joules
> (1,000 watt*hours = 3.6 million joules)
> 1 kWh (kilowatt hour) is the energy that is needed to light ten 100-watt light bulbs for 1 hour.

The principle that is used in all power plants for converting other kinds of energy into electric energy is very simple. We have seen that electric current can move a magnet (the needle of a compass). The converse is also true. A moving (rotating) magnet creates electric current in a closed circuit when the two are located in the right position relative to one other.

Different power stations convert different sources of energy into the kinetic energy of rotating magnets, which is converted into electric energy (which is used to "generate" electric current). (A power plant doesn't create electric charges; it only moves them.)

The most common sources of energy are the chemical energy of fossil fuels (mainly coal), the potential energy of water that is stored behind dams, and the (nuclear) energy stored in individual atoms that is converted into heat, which runs steam engines that move magnets. Recently the kinetic energy of wind and the energy of solar radiation are being used more and more as sources of energy for electric power.

Unit 12

Photovoltaic Cells

What Is a Photovoltaic Cell?

Photovoltaic cells are devices that use the energy of light (radiant energy) directly to create electric current (photo = light, voltaic = electric). They are also called solar cells.

Photovoltaic cells are used in solar-powered calculators and watches and in satellites and other human-made objects that are sent into space.

The principle is simple. Two thin layers of properly chosen transparent semiconductors (typically two different kinds of silicon) are put together. Light strikes the top layer.

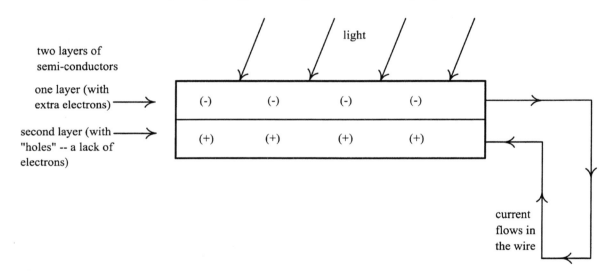

In a semiconductor, electrons can move, but not quite freely. The light rays hit electrons and displace them. When the semiconductors have the "right" properties, then the displaced electrons gather in one layer and avoid the other layer. Thus, one layer becomes negatively charged and the other layer becomes positively charged. In the picture, (-) means negative charges (electrons) gather in the top layer, and (+) means positive charges (a lack of electrons) gather in the bottom layer.

Now if you connect the layers with a wire, the current starts flowing from the top layer to the bottom layer. (This is the electricity that powers your TI-108 calculator.)

Efficiency

During a sunny day, solar light provides approximately 130 watts per square meter. Photovoltaic cells convert 6 percent to 13 percent of light energy into electric energy. Thus 1 square meter of photovoltaic cells provides power up to 17 watts.

With current technology, a cell must be used daily for approximately two years in order to produce the same amount of energy that was used to manufacture it.

Unit 13

Questions and Answers about Magnetism and Electricity

1. We note that the strength of one ring magnet is less than the strength of two, etc. But this relationship does not go up linearly. For example, if you double the number of magnets, you don't double the force. What is the relationship?
    We do not know any formula for it. We think that it may depend on several additional factors such as shape of the magnets.

2. (a) Can all magnets become demagnetized? Why or why not?
    Yes. Any magnet can be demagnetized, by heating it to a really high temperature, for example.

(b) Can you remagnetize a demagnetized magnet?
    It depends. Normally, yes. But a high temperature and cooling may change the arrangement of the atoms (e. g. by hardening the steel or by sudden cooling), and this may change the iron's ability to form a magnet.

3. Why do horseshoe magnets come with a little piece of metal across their two poles? What happens if you leave the metal off the horseshoe magnet?

Any magnet loses its magnetic property a little bit at a time.
Making a "closed" ring slows this process. In general the magnetic field of the magnet itself keeps its atoms aligned.
In an "open" horse shoe magnet, the lines of force inside of the magnet are close together, but they spread out at the poles.

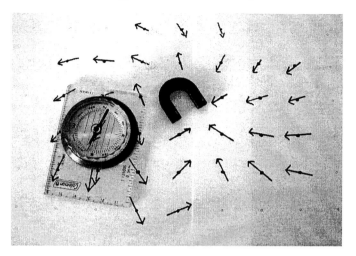

When you add an iron bar (called a "keeper"), then the lines of force go mainly inside the iron in a loop, which is better for keeping the atoms of the magnet aligned.

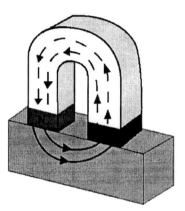

4. (a) What happens when you store compasses together in a box? How do they affect each other? Will some lose their "magnetic north" pointing ability?
We do not think that their being close would have such an influence.
Hot weather, their being shaken during transport, or just the passage of time are more likely causes.

(b) Same question for storing magnets together.
Here the answer is different. In this case, the magnets are strong enough to influence each other when they are stored together. If you store them in the same direction, they will keep better than a single magnet keeps alone.

But if you put them in the reverse direction:

Each magnet "tries" to reverse the direction of the other, and this may destroy the alignment of atoms in one or both of them.

5. If you magnetize a needle or nail with a magnet, does the magnet "lose" some of its magnetism to the needle or nail being magnetized?
   No. A magnet doesn't "give" anything to the needle. Its magnetic
   field aligns the atoms of the needle, turning the needle into a magnet.

6. Why doesn't a magnet point to the earth's "true" north rather than its "magnetic" north? What is "magnetic" north? Is it true that the earth's polarity switches occasionally?
   We think that the most current theory explains the earth's magnetic field as a field generated by electric currents deep in the earth. These currents are more or less perpendicular to the earth's axis, so the lines of force on the surface have a direction that is close to north-south. These lines "come together" close to the geographic poles. These points of convergence are magnetic poles. (At a magnetic pole, a "free" needle would point downward.) There is no known reason why the magnetic poles should coincide with geographic poles.

   Yes, it is well documented that the polarity changes occasionally, and what is more serious, that at the time of the switch, there is a short period when the earth has no magnetic field at all.

7. What is a "permanent" magnet? An "induced" magnet?
   Some pieces of iron preserve their magnetic properties almost indefinitely; some lose them fast (it depends on their internal structure and impurities). The first type are called permanent; the second type keep their properties as long as they are close to other magnets (an example is a nail touching a magnet), so they are called induced magnets.

8. Is there a simple way to state the relationship between electricity and magnetism? If so, how?
   Yes, and no. A simple answer is that electricity, magnetism, and also light are only different aspects of the same property of matter. But this "common core" of apparently different phenomena is understood only in terms of mathematical equations and doesn't have any intuitive appeal.

   Modern physics reduces the apparent infinity of different forces and interactions, to only four forces, which are related to four basic properties of matter:
   - the force of gravity, related to mass
   - the electromagnetic force, related to electric charge

- and two other forces, the strong and weak nuclear forces, which are related to properties of matter that manifest themselves only on the micro-scale of atoms.

9. Why does heating a magnet cause it to become demagnetized?
Atoms and chemical particles in solids are packed so they cannot move around (particles in liquids and gases can move). But particles in solids can shake and "dance" in place. We perceive this shaking as heat.

Particles become still only at a temperature of –273°C, which is the coldest possible temperature. (Nothing can be colder.)

In a magnet, the atoms of iron must stay aligned. But the more they shake, the bigger is the chance that they end up in a different position than they were before, and that they lose their alignment. This is the explanation for why heat demagnetizes magnets.

Chapter 10

Heat and Temperature

Unit 1

What Is Temperature?

Heat is a form of energy and, therefore, can be measured in joules. But traditionally it is measured in calories or kilocalories. A kilocalorie is very familiar because it used to measure the energy provided by the food we eat. (The prefix "kilo," which means 1,000, is then dropped). In scientific use, 1 calorie is written 1 cal, and 1 kilocalorie is written 1 kcal. Thus

$$1 \text{ kcal} = 1,000 \text{ cal}$$

One calorie is the amount of heat that raises the temperature of 1 gram of water by 1°C. Thus 1 kcal is the amount of heat needed to raise 1 kg (1 liter) of water by 1°C.

This means that we need approximately 70 kcal of heat to bring one quart of lukewarm water (at 30°C) to the boiling point of 100°C, in a covered pot. A cover is important because a lot of heat is "lost" due to the evaporation of heated water.

But What Is Temperature?

Modern physics explains temperature in terms of other physical processes that occur at the molecular level. But temperature is not defined in terms of the measurement of mass, length, time, and electric current. Therefore the unit of temperature, 1°C, is not defined in terms of kilograms, meters, seconds, and amperes; it is considered to be another basic unit of the International System of Units (SI).

In science, temperature is measured in Kelvins (1 Kelvin = 1° Kelvin = 1°C). The difference between Kelvins and degrees Celsius is in where the scale starts.

    0°C is the temperature at which water freezes
    0 Kelvin = –273.16°C

This temperature was chosen because it is the lowest possible temperature. Nothing in the universe can be colder than 0 Kelvin (0 K).

When you use the Celsius scale, the temperature can be positive or negative. In the Kelvin scale, you never have a negative temperature.

In everyday situations we measure temperature with thermometers. The principle involved is based on the fact that many substances (liquid or solid) expand when the temperature rises. In a usual thermometer we see the liquid rising or falling in a thin tube, depending on how much the liquid in the small container below expands or shrinks.

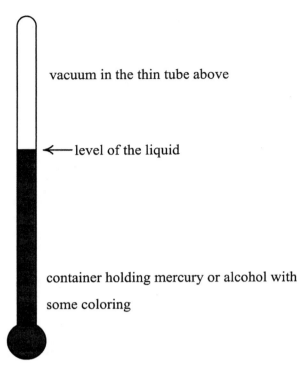

vacuum in the thin tube above

← level of the liquid

container holding mercury or alcohol with

some coloring

Measuring very high temperatures is based on the color of the light that is emitted (red-hot iron is cooler than white-hot iron).

Unit 2

The "Flow" of Heat

In experiments involving heat, water is the easiest to handle. We can carry out many experiments with water in a safe range of temperatures, and because of water's high heat-holding capacity, the precision of thermometers that are easily available is usually adequate. But even when we experiment with water, keeping its temperature constant is not easy. This difficulty is due to the properties of heat itself.

A Basic Property of Heat

When two substances come in contact, they exchange heat until they reach the same temperature.

We call this process the flow of heat. It is a spontaneous transfer of energy (heat) from the location of the higher temperature to the lower temperature. According to the basic heat equation, the change in the amount of heat is proportional to the change in temperature, so we observe what happens by seeing the decreasing difference of temperatures. Hot objects spontaneously cool, and cold objects heat up.

The word "flow" is used because people have made comparisons between heat transferring from higher to lower temperatures and water flowing from a higher to a lower elevation.

How Does Heat Travel?

In order to be able to keep a steady temperature during our experiments, we need to know the main ways of heat transfer.

Heat Conductivity

A simple experiment. You need a few cups: a metal cup (preferably an aluminum one), a plastic or a glass cup, and a styrofoam cup. Fill each of them with hot water and touch them. The aluminum cup feels very hot, the plastic one feels less hot, and the styrofoam cup is not hot at all.

Repeat the experiment with icy water. Again, the aluminum cup feels the coldest and the styrofoam cup is not cold at all.

These differences are due to the difference in heat conductivity of different substances. The heat flows fast through aluminum, and it flows very slowly through styrofoam. We say that aluminum is a good heat conductor and that styrofoam is a good insulator.

The amount of heat flowing also depends on other factors; the main one is the thickness of the insulation (the thicker the better) and the difference of temperatures on the two sides of the insulation (the flow is faster when the difference is bigger).

Convection

Convection is circulation of the air; it carries heat with it. Air is a good insulator, but it moves. A fluffy woolen sweater keeps you warm, as long as there is no wind. The air trapped between the fibers is a good insulator. But when the wind blows it away, you are exposed to a flow of cold air.

The most important factor in the cooling of hot water is evaporation. We know that the evaporation of 1 gram of water already takes about 540 calories.
The amount of evaporation depends on three main factors:
- The area of the surface of the water. (Bigger area→ more evaporation)
- The temperature. (Higher temperature→ more evaporation)
- The amount of water vapor in the air. (Dry air→ more evaporation)

If you keep water cold, below room temperature, the evaporation is too slow to matter. But if you want to use hot water around 90°C, evaporation becomes the main factor, causing a very fast drop in temperature.

In order to prevent fast cooling:
- Use containers with small openings.
- Keep containers tightly covered.

A small opening keeps the surface of the water small; a cover prevents the steam from escaping by convection and, therefore, keeps the vapor content of the air high, which prevents more evaporation.

Experiment

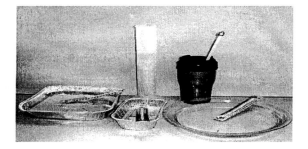

Put the same amount of very hot water in different containers (flat and shallow, tall and narrow, open, tightly covered). Measure the temperature every few minutes to see which one cools the slowest.

Radiation

This is a very important way of heat transfer. But it is only significant when the heat source has a really high temperature. This is the way the sun heats the earth, and the way we are warmed up when we sit next to a hot fire. In the experiments with water that are done mainly in a range between 0° and 90°C, the other methods of heat transfer play a much bigger role.

The Role of the Amount of Water That Is Used in Experiments

All methods of heat transfer depend on the surface area, but the amount of heat that is stored in a substance depends on its mass, which is proportional to its volume. Therefore, if the ratio of the surface area to the volume is small, then the loss or gain of heat during a given time would be a small fraction of the total heat that is stored. This means (on the basis of the basic heat equation; see previous unit) that the change of temperature would also be small.

Thus, errors in measurement due to (unavoidable) heat transfer during an experiment, in an environment that we cannot completely control, can be made small if we experiment with large amounts of water.

Remarks

1. Some compromise is needed because working with large volumes of water (let's say one gallon per table) can create a big mess. But sometimes it is better not to perform an experiment at all, than to perform it under conditions in which the results are unreliable.
2. Some experiments involve heat and can be done with a small amount of water. They deal with freezing and melting of fresh and salty water; however, they do not deal with the basic questions of storing heat and heat transfer, but with properties of different chemical substances.

Unit 3

Basic Facts about Heat and Temperature

To plan a good experiment, we need experience and some basic knowledge. We need to control the environment in order to minimize its influence on the variables we measure, and this requires a knowledge of which factors are important and which are not.

The Basic Heat Equation

When the temperature of some substance such as water or wood changes, then the difference of the heat inside the substance also changes. The equation below describes the relationship among the relevant variables and constants.

$$h = c * m * (T_2 - T_1)$$

- h is the amount of heat gained or lost (the change in the amount of heat that is stored in the substance)
- $T_2 - T_1$ is the difference between the final temperature and the initial temperature of the substance
- m is the mass of the substance
- c is the coefficient of heat capacity (specific heat). It is the amount of heat needed to increase the temperature of one unit of mass by one degree.

Units of Measurement

Heat is traditionally measured in calories (cal). It is a form of energy, so it can also be measured in any other unit used for measuring work.

$$1 \text{ cal} = 4.1868 \text{ joules}$$

The amount of chemical energy of food is also measured in "calories" for nutritional purposes. But these food calories are equal to the kilocalories (kcal) that are used in science.

$$
\begin{aligned}
1 \text{ food calorie} &= 1 \text{ kcal} \\
&= 1{,}000 \text{ cal} \\
&= 4{,}186.8 \text{ joules}
\end{aligned}
$$

The difference of temperatures is measured in Kelvins (K). Because 1 K = 1°C, T_1 and T_2 can both be measured in degrees Celsius. So the unit is:

> 1 Kelvin

Mass is measured in grams (g) or kilograms (kg). We will use:

> 1 gram

The coefficient of heat capacity (specific heat) is measured in (unnamed) units:

> 1 cal/g/K (one calorie per gram per Kelvin)

Remark

1. If you use other units, such as ounces, degrees Fahrenheit, and so on, convert them to metric before using them in the equation above.

The Coefficient of the Heat Capacity of Water

For water, the coefficient c is:

> c = 1 cal/g/K

This is a very big coefficient. Most substances around us have much smaller capabilities to store heat. So water is a rather special substance. Because c = 1, the basic equation applied to water is numerically simple. But if you forget about c, the dimensions of the left and right sides of the equation will not match.

Example 1

350 grams of water were heated from a temperature of 23°C to a temperature of 94°C. How much heat did the water absorb? (Give the answer in joules.)

> 94°C – 23°C = 71°C = 71 K, so
> h = (1 cal/g/K) * (350 g) * (71 K)
>   = (1 * 350 * 71) (cal/g/K)gK
>   = 24,850 cal
>   = 24,650 * 4.1868 joules
>   = 104,042 joules

Answer: 104,000 joules of heat were absorbed by the water.

Example 2

100 grams of water cooled from the boiling point (100°C) to a lukewarm temperature of 40°C. How much heat did the water lose?

$40°C - 100°C = -60$ K,
$h = 100 * (-60) = -6,000$ cal
(The minus sign shows that heat was lost, not gained.)

Answer: The water lost 6 kilocalories.

Some Limitations in Using the Basic Equation

The heat capacity of matter depends not only on its chemical composition, but also on its state: solid, liquid, or gaseous. Thus, for water, we can use the basic equation only within the range of 0°C to 100°C (where water is liquid).

The Heat Needed for Melting and Evaporation

The transition from one state of matter to another requires heat. Melting 1 gram of ice—changing 1 gram of ice at a temperature of 0°C into one gram of water at the same temperature—requires approximately 80 calories. Freezing water releases the same 80 calories per gram without any change in temperature.

Even more heat is needed for evaporation. To change 1 gram of water into steam at the same temperature requires approximately 540 calories. In reverse, condensation of 1 gram of steam back into water releases back the same 540 calories.

Remarks

1. This "energy carrying" property of steam was, and still is, used in steam engines. A coal (or other fuel) stove boils and evaporates water. The hot steam carries a lot of energy. This energy is used to move the pistons in a steam engine, or the wheel of a steam turbine. In this process the steam cools down and condenses, and most of its energy (including the 540 calories per gram that were used for evaporation) is converted into the kinetic energy of the pistons of the steam engine or the wheel of the turbine.
2. The specific heat of a substance is the amount of heat needed to raise the temperature of a unit of mass (for example, 1 gram) 1°C (or 1 Kelvin). Here is a table of the specific heat of some substances.

Material	Specific Heat (cal/g/K)	Material	Specific Heat cal/g/K
water	1.00	table salt	0.200
ice	0.50	hamburger	0.750
air	0.24	mercury	0.033
wood	0.42	steel	0.110
glass	0.20	aluminum	0.210
sand	0.20	gold	0.032

Unit 4

Experiments with Heat

Mixing Water of Different Temperatures

Task

You need to have two containers of water. In one container you have m_1 grams of water (450 g) at a temperature of T_1 close to 90°C. In the other container you have m_2 grams of water (320 g) at a temperature T_2 close to 0°C, but with no ice cubes in it.

Mix together well the water from both containers, and immediately measure the temperature T_3 of the mixture. Weigh the mixture to be sure that no water was spilled, or that the weights were in error. Record the data:

first container		second container		mixture	
m_1	T_1	m_2	T_2	m_3	T_3

Repeat this experiment, varying the amounts and temperatures, and compare the results with the results that other groups of students find.

Theoretical Prediction

Choose a "baseline" temperature T_0 between 0°C and 100°C.

Using the basic equation, find the amount of heat (in calories) that is in each container above (or below) what the same amount of water would have at the "baseline" temperature. From the basic equation:

$$h_1 = c * m_1 * (T_1 - T_0)$$
$$h_2 = c * m_2 * (T_2 - T_0)$$
$$c = 1 \text{ cal/g/K}$$

If there were no significant flow of energy to the environment (such as cooling by evaporation, etc.), then the amount of heat (energy) h_3 in the mixture would be

$$h_3 = h_1 + h_2 \text{ (and also } m_3 = m_1 + m_2 \text{)}$$

But

$$h_3 = c * m_3 * (T_3 - T_0) = c * (m_1 + m_2) * (T_3 - T_0)$$

Thus, we can find T_3 by solving the equation:

$$c * (m_1 + m_2) * (T_3 - T_0) = c * m_1 * (T_1 - T_0) + c * m_2 * (T_2 - T_0)$$

Solution

$$T_3 = T_0 + [m_1 * (T_1 - T_0) + m_2 * (T_2 - T_0)] / (m_1 + m_2)$$

Or after further simplification:

$$T_3 = (m_1 * T_1 + m_2 * T_2) / (m_1 + m_2) \text{ (Notice that this is a "weighted" average.)}$$

Analysis of Results

If $m_3 \neq m_1 + m_2$, then either water was spilled or the weighing was incorrect. The difference between the theoretical and observed T_3 is due to heat transfer to the environment (e.g., if you poured water into the third container, the container's temperature influenced the result; or pouring the hot water cooled it).

An Example (with Ideal Data)

$m_1 = 400$ g, $T_1 = 90°C$
$m_2 = 200$ g, $T_2 = 30°C$

We choose $T_0 = 20°C$ $\qquad T_1 - T_0 = 70$ K $\qquad T_2 - T_0 = 10$ K

$h_1 = (1 \text{ cal/g/K}) * (400 \text{ g}) * (70 \text{ K}) = 28,000$ cal
$h_2 = (1 \text{ cal/g/K}) * (200 \text{ g}) * (10 \text{ K}) = 2,000$ cal

$m_3 = m_1 + m_2 = 600$ g
$h_3 = h_1 + h_2 = 30,000$ cal

Because $h_3 = c * m_3 * (T_3 - T_0)$, we have $30,000 = 1 * 600 * (T_3 - 2_0)$.

So after cancellation, $50 = T_3 - 20$

Therefore, the temperature of the mixture should be $T_3 = 70°C$.

Remark

1. You can get the same value by plugging the numbers into the last formula for T_3, without computing h_1, h_2, and h_3.

Unit 5

Melting Ice

We said that it takes approximately 80 calories to melt 1 gram of ice at 0°C in order to get 1 gram of water at the same temperature. What experiment allows us to measure this "melting heat"?

Experiment

Use m_1 grams of hot water in a well-insulated container. It is better if the amount is large, maybe 1 liter. (You can use a half-gallon milk carton wrapped in several layers of newspaper.)

Measure the temperature of the water. Weigh m_2 grams of ice cubes or crushed ice; m_2 should be approximately $0.2 * m_1$, 20 percent of the weight of the water. (In order to fit in the spout of the milk carton, the ice will need to be in small pieces.) Keep the container covered. Wait until the ice melts and measure the temperature again.

Theory

- $T_0 = 0°C$ "Baseline" temperature, which is also the temperature of ice that comes out of the freezer
- T_1 Temperature of the hot water before the ice is added

- T_2 Temperature of the water after the ice has melted
- m_1 Mass of the water in grams
- m_2 Mass of the ice in grams
- x   Unknown amount of heat needed to melt 1 gram of ice, measured in cal/g ("melting heat")

If there were no loss (or gain) of energy to the environment, we would have:

(1) Amount of heat (over its amount at the baseline temperature) at the time when the ice is added.

Water: $h_1 = c * m_1 * (T_1 - T_0) = c * m_1 * T_1$

Ice: 0 cal (because it is at the "baseline" temperature)

                $T_0 = 0°C$

Total: $c * m_1 * T_1$

(2) Amount of heat (over its amount at the baseline temperature) after the ice has melted.

Water: $h_2 = c * (m_1 + m_2) * (T_2 - T_0) = c * (m_1 + m_2) * T_2$

Heat that
melted
the ice: $x * m_2$

Total: $c * (m_1 + m_2) * T_2 + x * m_2$

These two totals are equal (if there was no heat exchange with the environment) and, therefore:

$$c * m_1 * T_1 = c * (m_1 + m_2) T_2 + x * m_2$$

Thus,

$$x = c * (m_1 / m_2) * (T_1 - T_2) - c * T_2$$

An Example with Almost Ideal Data

We have:

$m_1 = 1000$ g of water at $T_1 = 90°C$

$m_2 = 200$ g of crushed ice at $0°C$

After the ice melted the temperature was:

$T_2 = 62°C$

We know that $c = 1$ cal/g/K

Thus:

$$x = 1 * 1,000 / 200 * (90 - 62) - 1 * 62 = 78 \text{ cal/g}$$

Remark

1. You may wonder where the heat that was used to melt the ice is "hiding." It is hiding in the molecular structure of water as compared to the molecular structure of ice. When the water starts freezing again at 0°C, this energy will be released back into the environment. Until then, it is "locked up" in water, and we have no access to it.

Unit 6

Energy Requirements for a Household and for a Human

Which is greater, the energy required by my body or the energy required by my house?

Let's find the answer for the month of April 2003. We will compare the food energy I needed and the gas and electricity that my house (occupied by one person) used. (We will not include other energy sources that my body used, such as transportation.)

My body requires about 2,000 calories (kilocalories) per day. 1 calorie = 4,184 joules, so 2,000 calories/day = 8,368,000 joules/day that I need for my body.

From March 25 to April 24, 2003, my house used 347 kilowatt hours (kwh) of electricity. (See the bill.) The amount of natural gas used in my house for the month ending April 22, 2003, was 3 dekatherms. (See the bill.)

```
┌─────────────────────────────────────────────────────────────────────────────┐
│         DATE                          NAME                                     │
│        4/29/03                                                                 │
│     ACCOUNT NUMBER                    SERVICE ADDRESS                           │
│                                                    LAS  CRUCES  NM    88011     │
│  TYPE OF    DATES          READINGS                                            │
│  SERVICE  PREVIOUS PRESENT PREVIOUS PRESENT MULTIPLIER   USAGE        AMOUNT    │
│  RESIDENTIAL CUSTOMER CHARGE                                         $6.00      │
│  RES.      3/25   4/24  62376  62723      1      347 ACTUAL KWH                 │
│                                                                                │
│                         ENERGY CHARGE*                              31.83       │
│                                                                                │
│                         TAX                                          2.46       │
│                                                              ------------       │
│                         CURRENT CHARGES                            40.29        │
│                         FIXED FUEL FACTOR:    347 KWH @ $0.00421                │
│                                     INCLUDES APPLICABLE TAXES        1.55       │
│                                                                                │
│                    TOTAL AMOUNT DUE BEFORE   5/21/03              $41.84        │
│           YOUR LAST PAYMENT OF        $42.25 WAS RECEIVED ON   4/09/03.         │
│           PAYMENTS RECEIVED AFTER   4/29/03 ARE NOT REFLECTED ON THIS BILL.     │
│                                                                                │
│           YOUR BILL INCLUDES A 2% FRANCHISE FEE ASSESSED BY CITY OF LAS CRUCES.│
│    *THE ENERGY PORTION OF YOUR BILL IS COMPOSED OF THE FOLLOWING FACTORS:       │
│                         ENERGY                                                  │
│           GENERATION    $0.06285/KWH                                            │
│           TRANSMISSION  $0.00451/KWH                                            │
│           DISTRIBUTION  $0.02437/KWH                                            │
│           TOTAL         $0.09173/KWH                                            │
└─────────────────────────────────────────────────────────────────────────────┘
```

First ,we compute the amount of joules per day for the electricity in my house.

347 kwh/30 days ≈ 11.6 kwh/day
1 kwh = 3,600,000 joules

So, the electricity used by my house for one day is approximately:
3,600,000 joules/kwh * 11.6 kwh/day = 41,760,000 joules/day

So, my house used almost five times as much energy for electricity as my body used.

● Development Fees				
Outstanding Balance:			Current Charges:	

Water Development Fees	0.00	
Wastewater Development Fees	0.00	
Total Outstanding Balance	0.00	

Current Charges:	
Water Principal..................................	0.00
Water Interest..................................	0.00
Wastewater Principal...........................	0.00
Wastewater Interest............................	0.00
● Total Charges for Development Fees	

● Gas Service

Billing Period Read Date	Rate Class		Meter Number	Current Reading	Previous Reading	Dekatherms Used
April 22	0101		4721961	706	703	3

Current Charges: * Mcf conversion to dth factor   0.899000

Monthly Fee...................................			7.99
Cost of Gas.___3___ __4.1362__..................			12.41
Cost of Service Charge ___3___ __1.3700__			4.11
Next ___0___ __0.0000__			0.00
Next ___0___ __0.0000__			0.00
Next ___0___ __0.0000__			0.00
Next ___0___ __0.0000__			0.00
Next ___0___ __0.0000__			0.00
Gas Service Gross Receipts Tax.................			1.59
● Total Charges for Gas Service.................			26.10

Now let's compute the joules per day for the natural gas used in my house.

3 dekatherms/month / 30 days/month = 0.1 dekatherm/day
1 BTU = 1,055 joules
1 therm = 100,000 BTU
1 dekatherm = 10 therms
0.1 dekatherm = 1 therm = 100,000 BTUs
100,000 BTUs/day * 1,055 joules/BTU = 105,500,000 joules/day for gas

So, my house used about 12.6 times as much energy for gas as my body used.

My house used about 147,260,000 joules of energy per day for its gas and electricity
My body used only 8,368,000 joules per day or about 5.7 percent as much as my house.

Electrical power is the rate at which an object uses electrical energy or at which it converts electrical energy into other forms of energy (for example, heat, light, and mechanical energy). Power is typically measured in watts. One watt is one joule/second.

We can compute how many watts of power my body demonstrates, on average, throughout a day. There are 86,400 seconds in one day. So my body demonstrates 8,368,000 joules/86,400 seconds ≈ 96.9 ≈ 100 watts (or joules/second). This is the same amount of power needed for a 100-watt light bulb that burns 24 hours per day.

Chapter 11

Hydrostatics and Hydrodynamics

Unit 1 Flow of Water

Unit 2 Inverted Glass of Water

Unit 3 Explanation for the Inverted Glass of Water Phenomenon

Unit 1

Flow of Water

Hydrostatics is the study of the distribution of pressure in stationary water or in a similar liquid. Hydrodynamics studies moving water and the forces interacting between water and objects that are swimming such as fish.

Units

We can measure the flow of water in a pipe in milliliters per second. One milliliter = 0.001 liter, and it is also one cubic centimeter of any liquid. The milliliter is a convenient unit when the amount of liquid is small. (One milliliter of pure water weighs 1 gram.)

Question

When water flows through a pipe (here: a rather thin, flexible hose) under the force of gravity, how does its flow depend on the height?

Experiment

Materials

Students work in groups of two to four. Each group needs:
- calibrated beaker or measuring cup
- piece of flexible hose at least one meter long (ours was made of clear plastic)
- stopwatch
- meter stick or tape measure
- pan or large dish for holding water
- For the data, paper, pencil, calculator, and graph paper are needed.

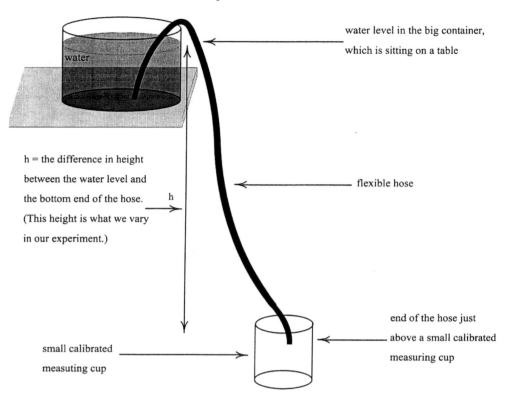

1. The top container must be big ~~enough~~ that the water level doesn't drop much while the measuring cup fills.
2. The hose should be flexible. How it coils doesn't matter, as long as it doesn't get "kinks." It should be narrow enough so that the time it takes to fill the measuring cup can be measured precisely.
3. The height is measured between the level of water in the top container and the end of the hose just above the measuring cup.
4. The top end of the hose may lie flat at the bottom of the container, but the lower end should be kept straight down.

Remark

1. You can also weigh the water and measure its flow in grams per second. (The numerical values would be the same if the measurements were exact.)

Variables

- h   measured in cm. (see picture)
- V   the volume of water in the cup in ml
- t   time it takes to fill the measuring cup to a particular level, in seconds
- F(h) = V / t   flow as a function of h, measured in mL/s

Measure V and t for different values of h. Make a table for F(h) as a function of h. Graph the data points.

Here are some data from an experiment we conducted.

Measuring rate of flow of water from different heights			
h = the difference in height between the water level and the bottom end of the hose (centimeters)	V = volume of water that flowed into graduated cylinder (milliliters)	t= time it takes, in seconds	F(h) = V / t = flow as a function of h, measured in milliliters/second
26.5 cm.	250 mL	38.27 sec.	6.5 mL/sec.
60.5 cm.	250 mL	21.99 sec.	11.4 mL/sec.
93.5 cm.	250 mL	17.18 sec.	14.6 mL/sec.

We graphed these data using Excel:

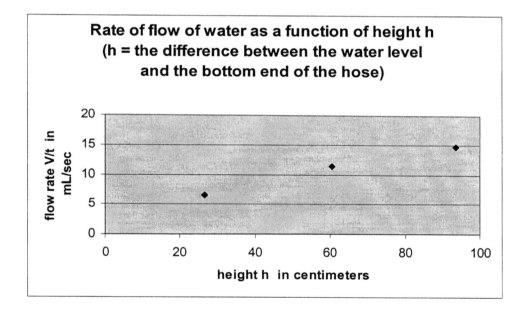

What conclusion can you draw? Is the function F(h) constant? Linear? Neither? Can you suggest a formula for F? Can you derive it from other facts that you know?

Our conclusion, based on the data above, is that flow rate increases as height increases. Our graph does not differ much from a straight line, but we cannot be sure that it is linear.

Unit 2

Inverted Glass of Water

Materials

This lesson must be done outdoors or over a large tub because water will spill. Students work in small groups. Each group should have:
- transparent plastic container
- transparent plastic glass
- plenty of water

Task

1. Fill the glass with water, but do not fill it to the very top. Put the container upside down on the glass as a lid.

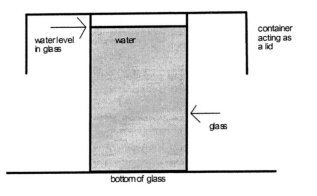

2. Using both hands, and holding the lid (the container) securely on the glass, turn the glass upside down.

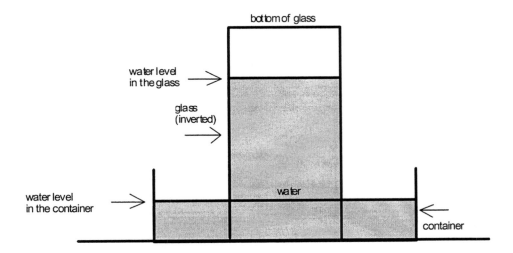

Water stays in the glass, which is turned upside down.

3. Add more water to the container.

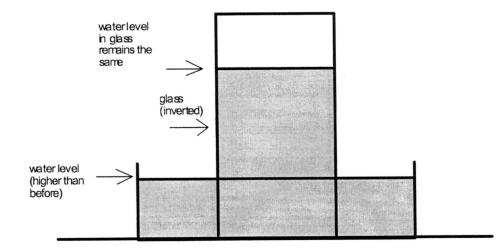

4. Slowly lift the glass up without taking its rim out of the water. What happens with the water level in the container? (See below.) You will notice that the glass feels heavy when you lift it.

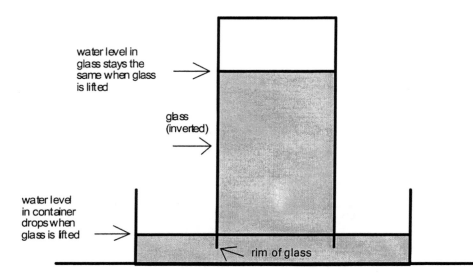

water level in
glass stays the
same when glass
is lifted →

glass
(inverted)
→

water level
in container
drops when
glass is lifted →

← rim of glass

When you lift the glass, the water in the glass is lifted with the glass, causing water to be sucked from the container. So, the water level in the container drops. When you lift the glass, it weighs as much as a full glass of water, not an empty one.

5. Lift the glass above the water level in the container. The water spills all over. What a mess! Explain what happened.

Unit 3

An Explanation for the Inverted Glass of Water Phenomenon

Pressure = force/area. The basic unit of pressure is the pascal.
1 pascal = 1 newton/square meter (1 newton is a force of about 3.6 ounces)
         = 0.000145 psi (pounds per square inch)

A pascal is a very small unit, so in practice other units are often used.
    For example, 1 bar = 100,000 pascals = 0.986923 atmospheres.
One bar is close to 1 kilogram of weight pressing on 1 square centimeter and to 14.7 psi (pounds per square inch). Atmospheric pressure, which is a measure of the pressure of air, is approximately 1 bar at low altitudes, but it changes with the weather.

The pressure of some amount of a gas depends on its volume. When the volume of a gas decreases, the pressure increases; but when gas expands, its pressure drops.

Under water, the pressure increases with increasing depth. It increases
    0.981 bar ≈ 1 bar
for each 10 meters under the surface of water. So the increase of pressure is proportional to the increase of the weight of a column of water above it.

In any connected body of liquid, the pressure at a given height is the same. (If the pressure would be different, the liquid would flow from higher pressure to lower pressure.) See the picture.

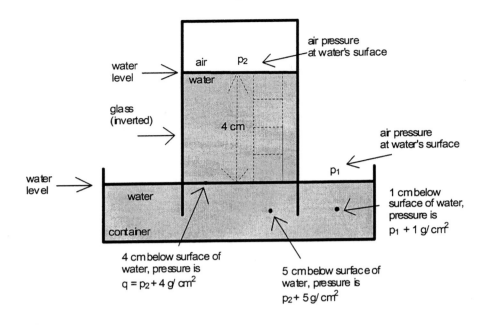

Let p_1 = air pressure on the outer container
Let p_2 = air pressure inside the glass

Let's say that the vertical distance from the water level inside the glass to the water level outside the glass is 4 cm.

Then $p_1 = p_2 + 4$ g/cm^2.
(4 g/cm2 are added due to the weight of the column of water, which is 4 cm. high.)

This equation is true because the two pressures, p_1 and $q = p_2 + 4$ g/cm^2, are at the same height (on the same level) in a connected body. (q is the sum of two pressures, p_2, which is the air pressure inside the glass, and 4 g/cm2, the pressure of the water above it. Note that water weighs 1 gram per cubic centimeter, so a column of 4 cm3 of water, 4 cm. high, adds 4 g/cm2 to the pressure.)

So $p_1 \approx 1$ kilogram/cm^2, i.e., p1 $\approx$ 1 atmosphere.
        p_2 is 4 grams less per square cm.
So $p_2 \approx 0.4\%$ (4/1,000) less than p_1. (There are 1,000 grams in a kilogram.)

If I have some air in an enclosed space, and the space is made larger or smaller (while the temperature remains the same), then the air pressure is inversely proportional to the volume. So, for example, if I double the volume, the pressure halves. If I decrease the volume to 50 percent, the pressure doubles. This works both ways: If I change the pressure, I change the volume; and vice versa.

So if the water level inside the glass drops down just a little, say from 4 cm. to 3.9 cm., then the pressure of the air inside the glass (call it p_3) will be smaller. (See the picture below.)

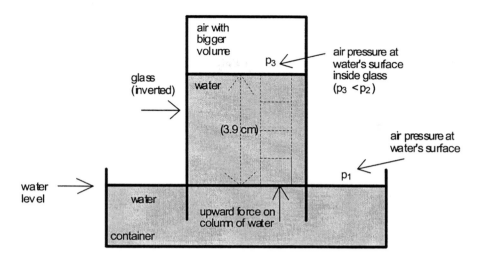

If this happens, then

$p_1 \; (= p_2) > p_3 + 3.9$ grams of water/cm^2.

But then there is a net upward force on the column of water, and the water moves up in the glass until p_3 becomes equal to p_2, that is, until the air pressure p_3 returns to the original air pressure p_2.

The air in the glass acts on the water in the glass just like a spring acts on an object that is hanging from it. When the water is disturbed, the water level returns to its previous level.

When you raise the glass above the water line, air bubbles start going into the water, and water spills out. If you put aluminum foil over the mouth of the glass before raising it, the water won't go out.

Another Experiment

Use a deep container filled about two-thirds with water, a clear glass, and a cork. Float the cork in the water, and place the (empty) inverted glass over the cork. Press the glass down to the bottom of the container. Can you explain what happens?

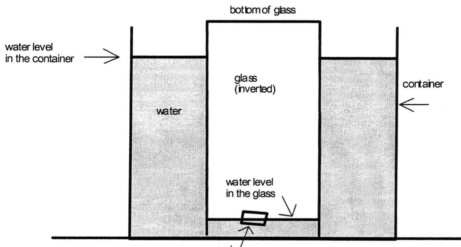

Chapter 12

Light

Unit 1

Does Light Travel in a Straight Line?

When you draw a straight line, you use a ruler. But for surveyors, straight lines are "lines of sight." And a "line of sight" is the path that light travels from an object to the eye.

In many situations the question "What is a straight line?" can be answered. "A straight line is a line that a ray of light follows." But the situation is more complex.

When light passes from one medium to another, for example, from air to water, from water to glass, and so on, it often changes direction.

But a different "optical" medium doesn't have to be a different substance. For example, hot air and cold air have slightly different optical properties. So, light may slightly change its direction passing from one layer of air to another. This is the reason for the "wet pavement" or mirage illusion that is often seen on highways during hot days.

The force of gravity also influences the direction of light. But this phenomenon is so small that it is barely observable, even on a cosmic scale when light passes close to a very massive star.

So saying that "light travels in a straight line" is a big simplification of a complex phenomenon.

Task 1

Fill a soup bowl with water and put a straw or pencil in the water. Look at the straw from many different angles. Describe what you observe. Can you explain what you see?

Do the same thing with a clear glass of water. Describe what you see.

Task 2

Fill a glass with water. Keep it at eye level, put a straw or pencil in the glass vertically, and move the straw from side to side. Describe and try to explain what you see.

Objects under Water

Light entering or leaving water changes direction.

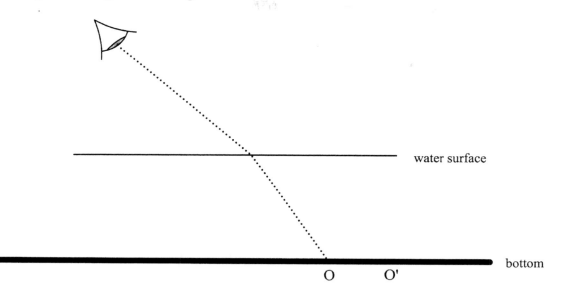

Thus, the light from an object O at the bottom travels to an eye of an observer along the dotted line, creating the impression the object is in position O′. This explains the "broken straw illusion."

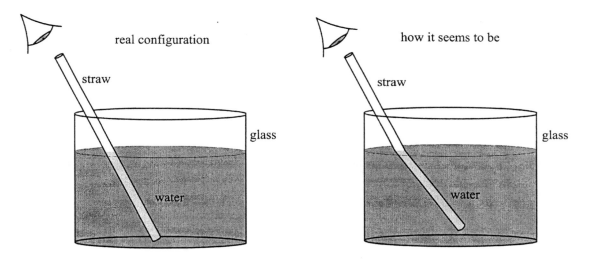

Notice also that container seems to be a little less deep than it really is.

Unit 2

Working with Mirrors

Materials

- small rectangular mirrors mounted on index cards (see picture), so they can stand in a vertical position on a table (we used 3 by 4 inch mirrors)
- Index cards (3 by 5 inch)
- colored markers
- tape
- compasses
- protractors

Students work in groups of four. Each group has three mirrors, along with the other supplies. Using colored markers, they should write several one- or two-digit numbers on index cards in large print. (One numbered index card per group is enough.) The numbers are going to be read through a system of mirrors.

Example

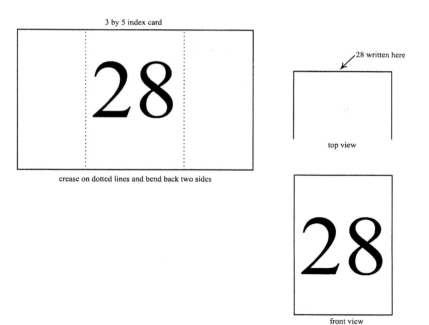

The cards will stand on a table, and they can be read only from one direction.

Task 1: Reading a Card with One Mirror

Mark the positions at the edge of the table where the card will stand, and where the observer will sit, with pennies attached to the table with tape. At the place where the mirror will stand, tape a sheet of paper to the table and mark a point on the piece of paper.

You have to put the mirror at such an angle that the observer can read the number in the mirror. The edge of the mirror must touch the point on the paper.

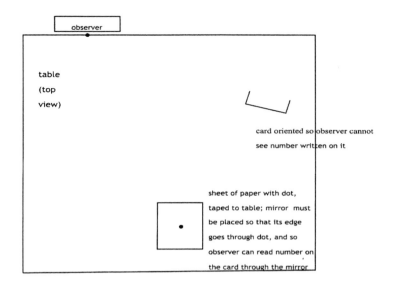

Task 2: Reading a Card with Two Mirrors

The situation is the same as above, except that there should be two places where the mirrors will stand (two pieces of paper taped to the table, with points marked on them), and the observer should see a reflection of a reflection.

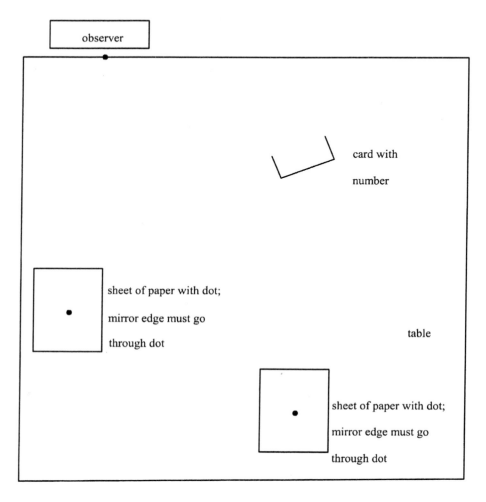

Task 3: Reading a Card with Three Mirrors

Again, the situation is the same as above, but with three reflections.

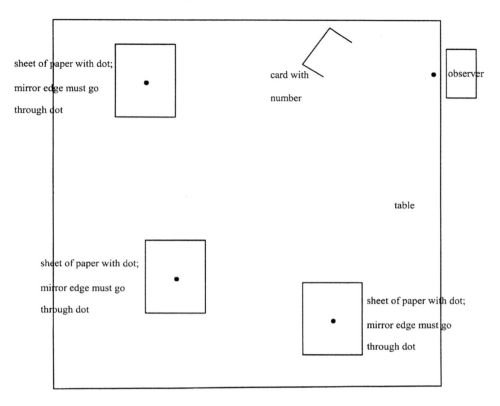

Theory

The angle of reflection of light from a mirror is the same as the angle of incidence.

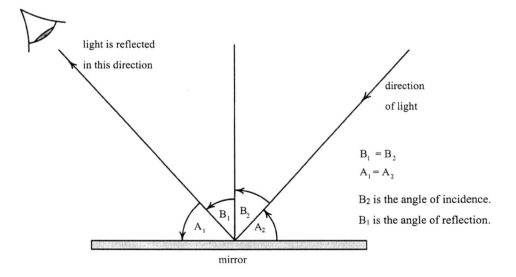

Thus, if you want to reflect light from P to Q by putting a mirror at R, you should aim from R to P and from R to Q, and draw straight lines in these directions. Then bisect angle C between them, and place the mirror perpendicular to the bisector.

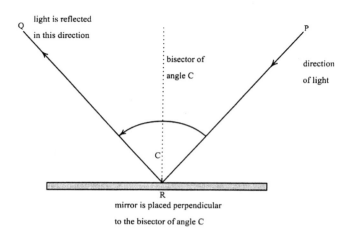

Remarks

1. The numbers reflected by one or three mirrors will be reversed. Young children may be surprised that some digits (0, 1, and 8) are not reversed.
2. The mirrors must be placed precisely. An error of one degree in placing the mirror leads to the following displacement of the image at a distance r:

$$2 * (2 * pi / 360) * r \approx 0.03 * r$$

This means that an error of 1° displaces the image by 3 cm. at a distance of 1 m. If you try to look at a reflection in three mirrors, the image can be moved out of your field of vision if you place the mirrors imprecisely.

About the Authors

Patricia Baggett has been professor of mathematical sciences at New Mexico State University since 1995. She earned her Ph.D. in psychology from the University of Colorado in 1977, and her main interests are how children and adults learn mathematics, and mathematics curriculum development.

Andrzej Ehrenfeucht has been professor of computer science at the University of Colorado since 1973. He earned his Ph.D. in mathematics in 1961, in Warsaw, Poland. His interests include the theory of computation and mathematical biology.